The Cloud Adoption Playbook

WITHDRAWN

The Cloud Adoption Playbook

Proven strategies for transforming your organization with the cloud

Moe Abdula
Ingo Averdunk
Roland Barcia
Kyle Brown
Ndu Emuchay

WILEY

The Cloud Adoption Playbook: Proven strategies for transforming your organization with the cloud

Published by
John Wiley & Sons, Inc.
10475 Crosspoint Boulevard
Indianapolis, IN 46256
www.wiley.com

© 2018, International Business Machines Corporation, Armonk, NY

Published simultaneously in Canada

ISBN: 978-1-119-49181-1

ISBN: 978-1-119-49185-9 (epub)

ISBN: 978-1-119-49183-5 (ePDF)

Manufactured in the United States of America

10 9 8 7 6 5 4 3 2 1

For general information on our other products and services please contact our Customer Care Department within the United States at (877) 762-2974, outside the United States at (317) 572-3993 or fax (317) 572-4002.

Wiley publishes in a variety of print and electronic formats and by print-on-demand. Some material included with standard print versions of this book may not be included in e-books or in print-on-demand. If this book refers to media such as a CD or DVD that is not included in the version you purchased, you may download this material at http://booksupport.wiley.com. For more information about Wiley products, visit www.wiley.com.

Library of Congress Control Number: 2018933540

Dedications

Moe: To my grandmother, a rock against which many leaned. Illiterate by circumstance, wisest by experience, she raised a tribe on her own. I also want to dedicate this to my family, *without* them there would be *no* me, really, gratitude.

Ingo: To my darling wife, Kathleen, and my sons Sebastian, Alex, and Leonard. You are important to me; I could not imagine a life without you.

Roland: All Glory to God the Father and My Lord Jesus Christ. As always, thanks to my wife, Blanca, for putting up with my schedule; I love you. I love my kids (Alyssa, Savvy, Joseph, and Amo); they rock.

Kyle: To my darling wife, Ann — thank you for putting up with yet another book project, even when you didn't think it was possible for me to be any more stressed out than I was. You're the greatest, dear.

Ndu: To my family, and especially to my brother Acho, whose memory lives on in our hearts.

About the Authors

Moe Abdula is one of the passionate and enthusiastic leaders of IBM's Cloud portfolio. As Vice President of the IBM Cloud Garage and Cloud Architecture and Solution Engineering, Moe leads a global practice of 13+ innovation Garages, powered by a team of Cloud solution, design thinking, enterprise delivery experts and distinguished engineers with focus on defining, implementing and enabling a key set of technology and industry patterns. During the last 20 years, Moe has held numerous development and field roles in IBM Software — most recently in Software Lifecycle Management, Operations Management and Mobile Platforms. Moe attended the University of Leeds in the UK, where he received an honors bachelor's degree in Electronic and Computer Engineering. Apart from contemplating clouds, Moe has passionate interests in football (soccer) and the unexpected experiences of life his two beautiful children drag him into!

Ingo Averdunk is an IBM Distinguished Engineer and leads the Cloud Service Management and Site Reliability Engineering practice in Cloud Adoption and Solution Engineering for IBM Cloud. He has more than twenty-five years of experience in enterprise systems and service management and consults with IBM's strategic customers globally. Ingo holds a masters degree in Computer Science and Theoretical Medicine at the Technical University of Munich (Germany) and is an ITIL Certified Service Manager. Ingo Averdunk is married to his wife Kathleen and a proud father of three sons. His main hobby is Karate, which he has practiced for more than 35 years.

Roland Barcia is an IBM Distinguished Engineer focused on IBM Cloud Private and CTO of Microservices, NYC Cloud Garage, and Solution Engineering in IBM Cloud Adoption and Solution Engineering. He is responsible for technical thought leadership and strategy, practice technical vitality, and technical enablement. He works with many enterprise clients on cloud strategy and implementations. He is the co-author of four books and has published more than 50 articles and papers on topics such as cloud technologies, Kubernetes, Microservices, Node, Containers, Java™, Ajax, REST, and messaging technologies. He frequently presents at conferences and to customers on various technologies. Roland has spent the past 18 years implementing cloud, mobile, API, middleware systems on various platforms, including Sockets, CORBA, Java EE, SOA, REST, web, mobile, and microservices architecture. He has a master's degree in computer science from the New Jersey Institute of Technology.

Kyle Brown is an IBM Distinguished Engineer and the CTO of Cloud Architectures for IBM Cloud Architectures and Solution Engineering. He has nearly 30 years of experience in building large-scale distributed and cloud-based systems. He is the co-developer of the IBM Cloud Garage Method and is responsible for the IBM Cloud Garage Method site and for the IBM Cloud Garage Architecture Center. He is an IBM Master Inventor with 17 US and foreign patents. He is the author of over 100 published articles, conducts web chats and Google Hangouts, records YouTube videos, and has written or contributed to ten books on software engineering topics, including this one. He holds a Masters Degree in Computer Engineering from North Carolina State University, a Bachelor's Degree in Computer Engineering from the University of Illinois at Urbana-Champaign, and is an avid runner.

Ndu Emuchay is the Global CTO, IBM Cloud Adoption and an IBM Distinguished Engineer, with extensive experience working with some of IBM's largest clients around the world and across industry. Ndu leads work on incubating next generation technologies, enabling the confluence and application of capability, expertise and experience in support of IBM clients, strategic IBM initiatives, thought leadership, and innovation. Over many years, Ndu's focus has been in working immersively with our clients and partners, driving solution design and technical leadership development to deliver business outcomes. Ndu holds a number of patents and is a member of IBM Academy of Technology. Ndu holds a Bachelor of Science degree and a Master of Science degree in Architecture & Design, and a Master of Science degree in Information Systems and Technology. Ndu lives in the Live Music Capital of the World — Austin, Texas; loves architecture, travel, music, food, culture, art and formula 1.

Credits

Acquisitions Editor: Steven Hayes

Project Manager: Colleen Diamond

Development Editor: Colleen Diamond

Copy Editor: Kathy Simpson

Technical Reviewers: Rachel Reinitz and Bobby Woolf

Editorial Assistant: Owen Kaelble

Production Editor: G. Vasanth Koilraj

Cover Design: Wiley

Cover Image: Courtesy of IBM, Inc.

Acknowledgments

Team: Special thanks go out to Sreekanth Iyer, who contributed much of the text for Chapter 6 — Sreek, you're the best — thank you so much for coming to our rescue when we needed you. Also special thanks to our technical reviewers, Rachel Reinitz and Bobby Woolf for spending hours over their holidays reading and commenting on this book. Special thanks also go out to Scott Shekerow for a completely unexpected but much appreciated editing pass on the early chapters of the book. We really appreciate it folks — thanks for your dedication and the sacrifice of your time.

Moe: A sincere thank you to my colleagues at IBM Lab Services and Cloud Garage, whose talented engagements at many clients and generous collaborations are reflected in our content. A special thank you to my friend and partner Bala Rajaraman, one of the greatest cloud minds and whose dedication and encouragement to truly master our craft, inspired much of our efforts.

Ingo: I want to thank my buddy and good friend Richard Wilkins (DE in IBM Singapore) for being my wingman when navigating through the stormy clouds. Richard — thanks for being available at odd hours to discuss technical approaches and challenges. Thanks also go to the solution engineers and consultants who validated the concepts in this book in the labs and with clients. Last but not least, I want to thank my wife Kathleen for allowing me to dedicate a majority of my time to clients and IBM.

Roland: Thank you to the many authors who contributed to the architecture center, which provided much content for us to use. Thank you to The Solution Engineers and Garage Method Team for the hard work and putting up with me.

Ndu: I'd like to thank the great talent I have had the privilege to cross paths with in life and work. I hope this book reflects in some important way the knowledge and wisdom our interaction has imparted to me.

Contents at a Glance

Contents

Foreword

By Steve Robinson, GM, IBM Hybrid Cloud

Over five years ago I took the opportunity to lead a startup team within IBM, which included some of the authors of this book, to develop a product that we thought would disrupt the industry. That product became IBM Bluemix PaaS, which is now at the heart of IBM Cloud. It certainly required disruption within IBM, as we had to build the product in ways that were transformational and new to us. It required us to move away from traditional models, and to learn how to develop natively for the cloud. We knew we had to embrace this new way of working to meet our clients' changing needs.

What I heard over and over again from our clients was that they needed to drive their own disruption, otherwise they risked being disrupted. If they didn't accelerate their own innovation, then a handful of programmers may just do it for them. They saw how agile organizations are disrupting industries and leaving established players in their wake like yesterday's business model. They knew they needed to innovate faster and bigger, at enterprise scale, to reap the benefits of industry disruption and market change.

For any enterprise, it was evident, change was inevitable. Transformation leveraging cloud as an underpinning of a new digital business was a requirement to survive. Understanding how best to adopt cloud leveraging tried and tested techniques was key to accelerating such transformation.

The challenge enterprises face is making this real. How do they accelerate innovation like a startup, have clear line of sight to users, and scale to the enterprise? Clients turned to us and asked how we transformed ourselves, and how we can help them do the same. They heard that we adopted agile and DevOps practices broadly with impressive results in velocity, and they wanted to know our secret sauce.

This need in the marketplace for enterprise transformation was the impetus for me to form another startup team (again with many of the authors of this book) focused on developing a different way of consulting with our clients. We became the IBM Cloud Garage.

Supported by proven methods and hardened architectures, the Garage captures the essence of a digital economy: maniacal focus on the client experience, minimum viable products with rapid iterations, modernization of existing systems, and equal emphasis on culture, processes, and tools.

When we opened the doors of the IBM Cloud Garage, we applied similar practices for our enterprise clients, showing them how to harness the energy of a startup culture and apply it to their organizations at scale. We've helped executives and developers alike achieve a culture of continuous innovation — resulting in faster delivery, time to market, and customer satisfaction.

What this group has done combines industry best practices on IBM Design Thinking, Lean Startup, Agile Development, and DevOps to help enterprise organizations adopt the cloud and accelerate all phases of the application design, development, and delivery lifecycle. This book captures that secret sauce of the Garage and the Cloud Architecture and Solution Engineering team into one reference, and shows you how to make the cloud real in an enterprise.

Steve Robinson
General Manager, Client Technical Engagement
IBM

Introduction

In a very real sense, the cloud is ubiquitous. We would find it hard to believe that there's a single reader of this book who doesn't consume some type of cloud service. Whether it be a cloud music service like Apple Music or Spotify, or cloud storage such as Dropbox, or a Software as a Service (SaaS) application like Salesforce running on the cloud, cloud services touch all our lives.

But these examples are just the tip of the proverbial iceberg. Cloud technologies such as Infrastructure as a Service (IaaS) and Platform as a Service (PaaS) are redefining how Information Technology (IT) organizations develop and deliver solutions to their customers. If you're an IT professional and you are not using the cloud in one of these ways already, you soon will be.

Who This Book Is For

Ever since Beal and Bohlen[1] defined the technology diffusion process in 1957, technologists have divided up the different waves of technology adopters into four different groups: Early Adopters, Early Majority, Majority (or Late Majority), and Laggards (or Non-Adopters). Those groups are often represented as different quartiles of a normal distribution or bell curve, as Figure I-1 shows[2]. Geoffrey Moore, in his classic book *Crossing the Chasm*, informed us that not all technologies make it past the Early Adopter stage; there's a large gap, or a "chasm" between Early Adopters and the Early Majority.

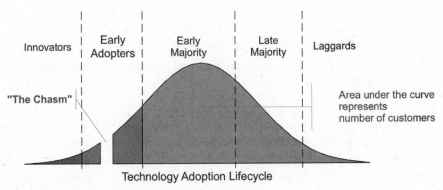

Figure I-1: Technology Adoption Curve.

What we can state, with finality, is that the cloud has made it past the technology adoption chasm. In a 2017 Forbes article[3], Louis Columbus quoted from an Intel survey that showed fully 80 percent of all IT budgets would be committed to cloud applications and solutions. The cloud has now clearly moved beyond the early adopters into the two majority quartiles.

That fact is what drove us to write this book. In our customer-facing work we have seen that the vast majority of IT departments, in all industries, are now facing the problem of deciding how to adopt cloud technologies, and are somewhere in the process of formulating strategies and approaches for how to go about changing their organizations to handle this new set of technologies. But what we have seen is that the process of formulating a successful cloud adoption strategy, and what's more, the process of implementing that strategy is not at all easy. What we will do in this book is show you how we have worked with many of the successful early adopters of the cloud and tell you their stories and share the lessons we have learned in working with them.

But we're not only writing this book to speak to the early majority and late majority of cloud adopters; we're writing it for a more specific audience — the enterprise audience. Our definition of an enterprise is simple; we mean a business that is not in the business of IT. So by this we exclude technology startups, which live in a different ecosystem and often work by different rules. If you are looking for tips and techniques on using the cloud to find your next round of venture capital, you're looking in the wrong place. However, if you work for an Insurance Company, a Bank, a Manufacturer, a Retailer, or any of the thousands of other businesses that use IT but aren't defined by IT, then you're a member of our core audience. The size of your business doesn't matter; we've worked with both large and small enterprises, and even startups, but the lessons that we present will be specifically tailored to helping you reach out to your most important stakeholders; your customers, both internal and external and transform that relationship to be more productive, responsive, and forward-looking by using the cloud as part of a larger ongoing digital transformation.

So whether you are the Chief Information Officer (CIO) or Chief Technology Officer (CTO) of an enterprise, or if you report to them in a more specific capacity such as Enterprise Architect, Chief Information Security Officer (CISO), Director of Engineering, or Director of Operations, this book is for you. In fact, we have written our chapters to speak specifically to each of those roles, as you will see later on. But this book is not only aimed at the C-Suite; if you work as a team member for any of the roles named above, you'll also gain valuable insight on how cloud will affect your job by reading this book.

Sports Analogies or the Lack Thereof

We have named this book *The Cloud Adoption Playbook*. There are two reasons for this; first, we're following in the footsteps of our friend and colleague Sanjeev Sharma, who wrote the *DevOps Adoption Playbook* in 2017. This book can be considered a companion volume to that book, as the two are complementary. You don't need to read Sanjeev's book to gain from this book but if you do read his book, and we recommend you do, you will learn a lot about many of the same subjects from a different perspective.

But the second reason is that we call this a playbook for the same reason that Sanjeev called his book a playbook. We're both drawing from the sports analogy where a playbook (in either basketball or American football) is the book that contains the plans and actions that a team carries out during a game.

Unlike Sanjeev's book, we're going to go super-light on the sports analogies; in fact, you'll not find another sports analogy beyond the introduction. But we do want to tell a story about an early sports playbook that inspired us. Glenn Scobey (Pop) Warner was an early American football coach that pioneered many of the precursors of modern American football plays. Much of his most innovative work was done at the tiny Carlisle Indian Industrial School where he was football coach at the turn of the 20th century. He was an expert at poring through the rulebooks and finding creative ways to bend the rules of football to allow his team to "punch above their weight". As a result, his team was able to beat teams from much larger colleges such as Columbia and Penn.

Warner's spirit of innovation is what inspired us. Cloud technologies and digital transformation hold the same promise; they can allow smaller enterprises to "punch above their weight" and can help make larger enterprises more nimble and agile. But sometimes you have to bend a few rules, or at least change the way in which your enterprise has traditionally done things in order to make that happen. Finding ways of dealing with the constant tension between innovation and the realities of working inside an enterprise will be one of the ongoing themes of this book.

What to Expect in Our Playbook

In Chapter 1, we will discuss the business drivers that lead enterprises to adopt cloud, as well as how elevated customer expectations drive new requirements that force you to the cloud. We will discuss how highly competitive environments are forcing organizations to move more quickly, and how the evolving regulatory-requirements landscape is also forcing change into existing organizations.

In Chapter 2, we will present an overview of our cloud adoption and transformation framework: its themes, the important dimensions along which an enterprise can gauge where it is and where it needs to be, and how it enables you to take a structured, holistic, and pragmatic approach to cloud adoption.

In Chapter 3, we will share our experience in developing a cloud adoption strategy, presenting the key attributes of such a strategy and providing a prescriptive approach to developing your own strategy. We will share examples of how other companies have developed such strategies and discuss the components of successful cloud adoption strategies.

In Chapter 4, we will focus on how cultural change is the basis for success with the cloud. Often, our clients tell us that cultural change is the most important and challenging aspect of cloud adoption and digital transformation. Culture directly relates to the most critical asset of your organization: your people.

In Chapter 5, we will describe a viewpoint on architecture and technology, showing you how new cloud platforms, service types, and programming models (such as microservices) offer potential competitive advantages. More importantly, we'll show you how to strike a balance between developing "architecture for architects" and how to communicate in the language of the developer.

In Chapter 6, we will discuss security, risk, and compliance. New technology approaches introduced by the cloud such as pooling and sharing of resources, new deployment models, and multivendor arrangements, mean that we must think differently about security, risk, and compliance. We'll show you how to take steps to keep up with rapid innovation while providing a safe, secure, and compliant environment for business.

In Chapter 7, we will discuss several technologies and trends that are having a profound effect on business and the technology platforms that support them. These emerging technologies are changing the nature of services available to your users. By the very nature of innovation, the only constant is change and learning how to deal with that change is the central theme of the chapter.

In Chapter 8, we will explore the IBM Cloud Garage Method that we have codified and refined over many client engagements and in our internal development at IBM. These codified insights and best practices are the keys to rapidly scaling an organization's capabilities. We'll discuss the origins of our approach, our lessons learned, and how a holistic view of practices from many different areas is required not only to develop solutions correctly, but to develop the correct solution.

In Chapter 9, we will focus on cloud service management and operations. We will discuss what management and management practices must look for in the cloud. This will include introducing new practices that we have developed and that we have seen work in some of the most challenging enterprise contexts.

In Chapter 10, we will introduce our views on governance. We cannot overstate the importance of governance, which provides the backdrop for effective execution of strategy and continuous advancement toward business outcomes.

The IBM Cloud Adoption Playbook will provide you not only with a conceptual framework for cloud adoption and digital transformation, but with a complete, structured, holistic, and pragmatic approach to succeeding on the cloud.

1 Business Drivers

The ongoing digital revolution affects individuals and businesses alike. Increasingly, social networks and digital devices are the default means for engaging government, businesses, and civil society, as well as friends and family members. People use mobile, interactive tools to determine who to trust, where to go, and what to buy. This means that the last best experience that people have anywhere becomes the minimum expectation for the experience they want everywhere, including in the enterprise. Given the competitive landscape, this means that enterprises must undertake their own digital transformations, rethink what their customers value most, and create operating models that take advantage of what is newly possible for competitive differentiation.

The challenge for the enterprise is how fast and how far to go down the path to digital transformation and cloud adoption.

Addressing Challenges for the Enterprise

To meet this challenge, enterprises must develop a methodical approach to embracing digital transformation and the cloud. Developing that approach means that they must answer questions such as:

- How do we situate such transformation in the complexity of the enterprise itself and the regulatory environment in which the enterprise operates?
- What considered, integrated set of decisions should we make to ensure consistency and safety at scale?
- How do we ascertain what success looks like in the short term, as well as what steps we need to take in the long term to sustain it?

Increasing customer expectations and a more competitive business context have placed tremendous pressure on business leaders to change the way they set their strategies and run their organizations. New requirements to incorporate more information and greater interactivity quickly drive up costs and complexity.

Business leaders have long used information technology to improve productivity and efficiency, reach new markets, and optimize supply chains. What is new is that customer expectations have changed. How can enterprises best respond to this shift? How can they take advantage of the opportunity to innovate and grow through technology adoption? And how can they do all this cost-efficiently?

This is the domain of digital transformation and its intersection with cloud adoption. Digital transformation incorporates the change associated with the application of digital technology in all aspects of society[1]. Cloud Adoption is the way in which businesses implement digital transformation.

In our work with clients, we have found that enterprises that can develop and effectively execute a digital transformation strategy and take full advantage of new technologies, such as cloud are able to transform their business models and set a new direction for entire industries.

We believe the most crucial decision that a company can make to successfully pursue a digital transformation strategy is to wholeheartedly yet thoughtfully adopt the cloud as the IT platform of choice. We have observed many companies that have successfully used cloud adoption to rapidly advance their digital transformation strategy. We have also seen companies make unsuccessful cloud adoption decisions that have hampered or set back their pace of digital transformation. What we will show you in this book is how to model your decision-making process after the successful transformations while avoiding the common pitfalls we've seen in the unsuccessful transformations.

We propose to show you how to do this by focusing on three areas:

- Think and Envision the Transformation
- Balance the Transformation
- Thrive on New Foundations

Along with insights from our direct consulting work with many industry-leading organizations, the ideas we present in *The Cloud Adoption Playbook* (the *Playbook*) are underscored by influential works including *The Three Laws of Performance,* by Steve Zaffron and Dave Logan[2]; *The Innovator's Dilemma,* by Clayton Christensen[3]; *View from the Top,* by Michael Lindsay[4]; and the transformation of IBM itself.

This *Playbook* is for those who are (or aspire to be) catalysts for digital transformation in their organizations; leaders who see the need for transformation as well as those who have direct responsibility for executing it. We intend to bridge the business and technology divide and provide a holistic but pragmatic set of ideas that can enable considered, consistent, and successful implementation within complex organizational constructs. We hope that this *Playbook* guides you in deciding how and where to get started in your digital transformation journey, what important dimensions to consider, and how to make integrated decisions that significantly improve the chances of success while reducing risk.

We have seen many cloud adoption and digital transformation programs succeed; we have also seen many fail. We hope that the tips in this *Playbook* will add to the body of knowledge and experience on replicating success and extending its impact.

What Drives a Business to the Cloud?

Technology in general, and the cloud specifically, are only a means to an end. The end needs to be defined in terms of a business or mission-strategic intent such as the following business drivers:

- Exceptional user experience
- Accelerated time to market
- Higher service quality
- Cost flexibility
- Repeatability and flexibility
- Safety, security, and compliance with regulation

Growing your business to meet these business drivers requires change and organizational transformation beyond just adoption of technology. To understand where cloud adoption and digital transformation fit within the enterprise, you have to place them within the context of very complex organizational constructs requiring a holistic approach. This approach needs to take into account the requirement to make progress and show success in the short term while keeping the long-term goals in sharp focus.

Because of this organizational complexity, we must define what success looks like in this context to show you what refinement looks like and to demonstrate how to achieve quick wins along the way. The following questions can help guide your organization in understanding this definition of success:

- What are our specific measures of success? Examples might include "Attract and retain top talent" or "Reduce IT delivery time by 15 percent."
- What are some quick wins in the short term that the cloud could help us achieve? Examples might include "Conduct a workload and data classification analysis to determine what workloads have affinity to the cloud and migrate 5 percent of those to cloud within one year" or "Deliver a high-profile pilot cloud-native application that opens a new route for customer interaction, such as a native mobile app or artificial-intelligence chatbot."
- What does sustainable success look like in the long term for our digital transformation journey? One example might be "Support idea to market rollout in less than one month."
- What are the key success factors that our whole organization needs to understand and march toward? One example might be "Improve customer experience by 5 percent on a continuous basis as measured by Net Promoter Score (NPS)."

Quick wins are powerful ways to secure and retain sponsorship. We have seen that companies gain more success over the long term when they build effective, enduring cloud transformation programs that aligned with their strategic intent and business drivers. We recommend that you take stock and periodically evaluate this alignment and course-adjust as necessary to achieve strategic outcomes.

We recognize that cloud technologies present an unprecedented potential for organizations to re-envision their relationship with information technology. But we also believe that the cloud is a catalyst to allow you to go well beyond re-envisioning to actual realization of new types of value. Cloud adoption can transform organizations by better empowering their workforces and ultimately differentiating them from competitors. Companies that can tap this potential become disruptors in their respective markets regardless of industry, which represents a real opportunity for leaders of these organizations.

We also recognize that given their successful history and ongoing commitments with their most valued clients, organizations adopting the cloud may experience first-hand the *innovator's dilemma*. You have to strike a balance between two worlds: delivering on existing commitments to stakeholders employing traditional IT methods and tools, and simultaneously adopting the game-changing new technologies required to meet disruptive new business opportunities. All organizations must work out how far to go in each direction to decide what is right for them. In this *Playbook,* we provide practical approaches to the decisions that need to be made and ways to take action along the important decision-making dimensions we lay out.

What Do You Gain from Cloud?

According to the 2011 National Institute of Standards and Technology (NIST) definition, "Cloud computing is a model for enabling ubiquitous, convenient, on-demand network access to a shared pool of configurable computing resources (e.g., networks, servers, storage, applications, and services) that can be rapidly provisioned and released with minimal management effort or service provider interaction."

The practical outcomes that companies want to realize from cloud computing include resource elasticity, cost flexibility, and self-service provisioning. Putting these two together, you see that you need to achieve the outcomes by using the services provided by cloud providers. This requires a model that allows you to choose not only what services you want, but where they run, and what vendors or providers you purchase them from. We provide practical examples of these models throughout the book.

Taking a step back and looking at the business intents behind why customer adopt cloud, we see enterprises taking advantage of the cloud model because it promises improved efficiency, expanded innovation potential, and revenue growth. We see technology and business function leaders alike attracted to the cloud for the value that it has the potential to deliver. Within these enterprises, leaders are aligning their cloud adoption and their digital transformation programs through strategic intents such as the following:

- **Creating a customer-focused enterprise:** This intent takes advantage of the cloud model to optimize data and use analytics to adapt to new user behaviors, cultivate trust, and drive profitable growth while preserving an exceptional user experience.
- **Increasing flexibility and streamlining operations:** You can use the cloud to improve operating leverage with variable cost structures that

increase flexibility for both the user and the provider of the cloud-based service. Furthermore, you need to provide higher-quality service, accelerate time to market, and reduce risk.

- **Driving innovation while managing cost:** By using the cloud to deliver new services efficiently, these new services can improve cost flexibility, provide users instant gratification, and drive competitive differentiation. But you must balance these improvements against decreasing cost per transaction and optimization of existing investments.

- **Optimizing enterprise risk management:** You can use the cloud to achieve compliance objectives and mitigate operational risk while maximizing return on equity; combating malicious activity; and incorporating repeatability, scalability, resiliency, and flexibility.

At the time of the 2011 NIST definition, cost reduction, improved data access, and demand generation were the top business drivers for cloud adoption. We have seen business drivers, technology platforms, services offered, and cloud deployment models evolve since that time. The top business drivers for cloud now include building exceptional user experiences, providing services in a multi-cloud hybrid environment, and modernizing applications to update existing Information Technology estates. Modernization is especially important for protecting your existing investment while opening applications and data up for new value delivery.

Enterprise digital transformation began with cost savings and simple lift-and-shift initiatives purely for efficiency. Efficiency is now a given, and enterprises require a multi-cloud, integrated platform to enable them to disrupt their industries and lead in their markets.

Although the cloud has helped early adopters generate innovation and new forms of collaboration, there is a concerted shift to scale cloud adoption across the enterprise. This shift includes addressing digital transformation in a sustained way, recognizing that some business functions are more amenable to cloud adoption than others.

Leveraging business drivers and strategic intent to guide and inform the way you rethink cloud adoption and digital transformation means maintaining alignment throughout the transformation journey. Your business is reinvented as the transformation occurs and accomplishments are achieved. The cloud becomes a true catalyst, generating momentum and creating a virtuous circle that creates sustained business success with expanded effect throughout the enterprise.

With your understanding of the intrinsic relationship between business and technology and the need to continuously strive for alignment through the techniques described in the *Playbook,* we believe that you will be much better positioned to achieve success in both the short term and the long term.

Implications to the Enterprise

Many of the ideas we describe in this book can and should apply to any organization, but we highlight the challenges that cloud adoption presents in large enterprises, particularly those that are involved in strategic outsourcing.

You need to understand the critical importance of the value that technology vendors and service providers deliver to enterprises — and, equally important, the rate of adoption and transformation within your enterprise. Although the *Playbook* assumes the perspective of the enterprise, for a fuller context, you must consider the service-provider relationships and contract vehicles through which such value is delivered to you.

Especially in strategic outsourcing arrangements, service providers earn their revenue by taking on risk on behalf of their clients. If you are in an arrangement like this, it means that you must take care to ensure that you factor in the commitments the service provider has made (including appropriate procedures, buffers, service level agreements, and checks) into how you realize the Playbook in real life. As a result, we recommend a holistic approach to transformation, taking into account time, relationships, organizations, assumptions, talent, culture, and other factors. Likewise, you need to take a pragmatic approach as you apply the tips in this book, one that recognizes where your organization is in their journey, that meets your organization where they are, and that guides the organization along the path of cloud adoption and digital transformation.

As you balance sustained innovation and disruptive innovation to keep pace with market forces and business priorities, the culture of care and risk-aversion typically comes into direct conflict with the need for rapid innovation. Our experience is that clearly outlined criteria along the dimensions of consideration enable decision-making for these types of trade-offs. Where you fall on the spectrum between sustained innovation and disruptive innovation and the decisions that you need to make depend on factors specific to your organization and your priorities. We address these important dimensions in Chapter 2 on the Framework and in later chapters.

We observe, especially in long-term strategic outsourcing arrangements, that enterprises see capabilities in the cloud that seem similar to — and cheaper than — what they're paying a lot of money for in their existing contracts. Enterprises also see many new possibilities in the cloud. These possibilities can be realized through cognitive capabilities; containers; prefabricated mobile application development environments; DevOps components; and a spectrum of useful services such as data analytics, machine learning, and artificial intelligence. These kinds of services are offered in a variety of cloud environments, and organizations are applying multi-cloud adoption strategies to take advantage of these services where they exist. Therefore, market pressure is growing to employ these powerful capabilities to deliver new value faster — and at scale.

These are just a few practical examples of how innovation changes the relationship between the service provider and the service consumer in the enterprise context. Our experience is that the implications of digital transformation can be quite wide reaching. In addition to innovating with technology, you need to innovate in your vendor contracts to capture the evolving relationship between the enterprise and the service provider. Further, you must incorporate these technologies into the new enterprise operating model in order to take full and meaningful advantage of these new possibilities. It will do you no good if your contract with your service provider makes you pay for services that are no longer needed because they have been replaced by newer cloud-based technologies, or that forces you to continue to provision services such as development environments manually when they can be instead directly requested through a self-service catalog.

You also must consider your enterprise's tolerance for sustained or disruptive innovation and how that innovation fits into its priorities. The process begins by clarifying your objectives. You must decide what you really want from digital transformation and cloud adoption. You must determine the strategic intent behind those objectives, determine how well aligned your enterprise is to those objectives, and continually re-evaluate what you must do to align with these objectives.

We see many tried-and-true business models being disrupted by cloud service providers and the services that they provide. This causes enterprises to react in a variety of ways; in many cases, the response has been to adopt multimodal IT; that is trying to segregate projects into "faster" and "slower" lanes to allow innovation on the cloud even as they seek alternative solutions.

What's more, lines of business that are pressed by market forces find themselves having to work around their internal IT providers. This is because the LOB's believe they need either responsiveness or capabilities beyond what internal IT has the capacity to offer. As a result, instead of internal IT acting as a trusted adviser and de facto service provider, others assume this role.

Summary

This chapter showed what drives businesses to the cloud, and what businesses can expect to gain from cloud adoption. This chapter also showed how the cloud can disrupt your current approaches and IT operations models — both internally and with outside vendors.

Digital transformation is not easy; it requires inspiration, a clear and consistent focus, and persistence over time. It also requires a playbook to help you understand all the different areas you need to consider and how they work together or come into conflict.

This leaves you, as a catalyst and a leader, in a challenging position. You need to be able to address the following questions:

- How do you articulate a holistic but pragmatic approach that takes organizational tensions into account and recognizes the need to move quickly and in a concerted, coordinated way?
- How do you decide where to start bringing key stakeholders to the table and charting a path that causes alignment?
- What are the steps you need to follow to significantly increase the chances of success while reducing risk to the enterprise?

We will explore the answers to these questions (and others) in Chapter 2.

2

Framework Overview

In this chapter, we introduce our approach for moving organizations into cloud-enabled digital transformation through an actionable framework that makes up the rest of the *Playbook*. We assembled this framework by mining insights from our extensive experience partnering with our largest enterprise clients. The framework is meant for leaders, catalysts, and key influencers who are looking to accelerate and replicate sustained transformative success in their organizations.

Throughout the Playbook we will reference examples of real clients from a variety of industries that have successfully navigated this kind of transformative journey. We will provide ongoing examples from three companies where we successfully applied the framework:

- We showed a global multinational bank headquartered in Europe how to reduce overall IT spend 21 percent over two years through a workload modernization and migration effort.
- We partnered with a global airline to deliver new applications in months rather than years, while at the same time moving their critical existing workloads onto the cloud, and fundamentally changing the way they performed service management on the cloud.
- We worked with a global building-materials manufacturing company to change its supply chain and order-to-cash processes to take advantage of an integrated digital platform, providing a seamless multi-device experience for placing orders, tracking shipments, and managing invoices and payments.

These examples demonstrate how the framework has been applied in practice — an approach that has guided decision-making and digital transformation road-map execution in a repeatable way and at scale.

Throughout the book, and specifically in the framework description, we will assume an outside-in perspective. The outside-in approach ensures that we are being client-centered as we apply the decisions in the framework. The most important thing to us is to make sure that we enable our client's success, which is more critical than following the rules or procedures of a framework. That perspective determined the structure of the framework by leading us to establish three simple themes that guide the decision-making process (see Figure 2-1):

- *Think and Envision the Transformation* **to establish the strategic intent of the transformation.** This step is the most important one. As we stated earlier, the cloud is a means to an end. First, you must determine what goals the business wants to achieve before you begin any other planning.
- *Balance the Transformation* **to decide what works best for the enterprise.** Just as Rome wasn't built in a day, an enterprise doesn't fully move onto the cloud in a day, or even in a year. There is always a balance that must be struck in understanding what aspects of the digital transformation you can move toward quickly and what parts will take more time.
- *Thrive on New Foundations* **to realize the strategic outcomes at scale and over a sustained period (typically, three to five years).** We want to help build organizations that are successful over the long run, which means going well beyond moving a single project to the cloud or transforming a single development team. To be successful over that time frame, you must establish organizational structures, policies, and procedures that are resilient and effective in the face of a rapidly changing technology landscape.

Figure 2-1: Framework themes.

Client strategic objectives anchor the framework and serve as guideposts to meet your organization where it is, and to chart a path to your future strategic outcomes.

The Framework

As we set the context and explore the framework elements in detail, we recognize that transformation is hard and needs to be given thoughtful consideration. Transformation involves much more than technology alone; people, process, information, and culture are other important factors. Therefore, cloud adoption and digital transformation come with challenges and exacerbate friction in existing constructs, which need to be addressed for successful outcomes. Following are some of these possible areas of friction (but by no means an exhaustive list):

- **Organizations moving to the cloud must make migration and modernization decisions to determine the best fit for existing applications and data.** The problem here is that whenever an application is selected to move to the cloud or stay on existing platforms, some people who are touched by that decision will disagree not on technical merits, but on how the decision affects them or their career goals.

- **Organizations require the right talent to fuel innovation and usually require organizational-culture upgrades to support new ways of working to achieve the intended velocity of change.** Personnel decisions always create conflict, however, as people find that the value placed on them by the organization based on their skills and abilities changes when organizational priorities change.

- **Organizations can encounter risks as tool selections made for traditional enterprise application development may not be the right ones for development for the cloud.** This situation not only affects the people in the organization who are responsible for the current tools, but also generates pressure from existing vendors whose revenue may be adversely affected. The parties often attempt to sow fear, uncertainty, and doubt about the validity of the planned transformation to protect their interests.

- **Organizations require a development methodology that is suited for both cloud-enabled and cloud-native development, as well as enabling management and delivery in a multicloud model at scale.** You can encounter resistance both from those who promote the existing enterprise methodology and those who promote competing new methodologies. Again, you can encounter pressure from cloud vendors who want to maximize their own revenue by suggesting that you move more to the public cloud than you may be ready to move. At the same time, on-premises hardware, software, and strategic-outsourcing vendors may push back from the opposite direction.

- **Organizations face operational challenges in integrating, managing, and securing off- and on-premises applications and data as a consistent whole.** We have often encountered friction between existing operations teams, which feel that cloud operations should fit into their current models and approaches, and newly established cloud development teams, which feel that they can conduct cloud operations on their own without the input of the existing operations team.

Our observation is that to overcome these challenges, organizations must do the following:

- Practice new forms of agile engagement and organizational alignment.
- Rethink and renegotiate relationships with providers.
- Establish new foundations (in terms of methods, tools, and skills) to propel transformation.

Upcoming chapters of the *Cloud Adoption Playbook* deal with these unique challenges and show how your organization can meet the new requirements.

For many IT organizations, the overarching goals include improving efficiency, complying with regulations, providing a secure environment for business transactions, and driving technology alignment with business objectives. All these goals require close collaboration and trust between the business and IT. We have found that achieving these goals requires IT organizations to ultimately reestablish and rebuild an effective relationship with their most valued stakeholders based on the new cloud paradigm.

We designed the framework to create an approachable model for cloud adoption and digital transformation. This framework can be used by organizations at many different cloud maturity levels to define a customized cloud adoption and digital transformation journey. The framework enables a conversation with stakeholders who must work together to deliver the value of transformation rooted in innovation. These stakeholders include IT leaders, developers, line-of-business executives, security experts and compliance officers, and service management and operation leaders.

In the chapters that follow, we will show you how to put yourself in the shoes of these stakeholders to help them understand the benefits, potential pitfalls, and guideposts of a successful cloud adoption.

Key dimensions of cloud adoption

The framework articulates our approach to addressing the key dimensions of cloud adoption and digital transformation. It incorporates our methodology for applying that structured approach and industry best practices for execution. The framework follows a flexible approach, which is pragmatic and meets the organization where it is. The framework will help you align your strategic intent with business outcomes and better align your business and technology. We believe that the framework can significantly improve the chances of measurable, visible success by helping you prioritize actions to deliver significant value to your organization.

Because cloud adoption and business transformation can have far-reaching effects across an organization, and because getting started on these projects can be quite daunting, the framework identifies several important dimensions to focus on (see Figure 2-2). These dimensions reflect what we see in our work with clients as having direct effects on a business. Note that these dimensions change and evolve over time, so the following list reflects current trends and is not intended to be exhaustive but to aid prioritization:

- Culture and organization
- Architecture and technology
- Security and compliance
- Emerging Innovation Spaces
- Methodology
- Service management and operations
- Governance

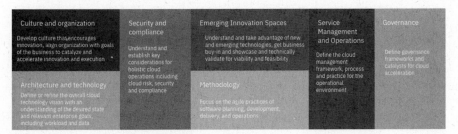

Figure 2-2: Dimensions of adoption.

These dimensions encapsulate the key areas of people, process, and technology that enterprises must change in order to be successful with cloud adoption and digital transformation. Each dimension is described in more detail with definitions in the succeeding Chapters 3-10 of the *Playbook*.

Steps in the adoption journey

Creating journey maps specific to your organization can help you achieve the outcomes you have defined. In a rapidly changing agile environment, starting quickly by understanding business need and evaluating the required capabilities is the first stage of your journey. Proving and validating those ideas quickly and scaling quickly become the next stages of the journey of cloud adoption and digital transformation.

To accomplish this in an iterative, consistent way, we recommend the following steps (see Figure 2-3):

Figure 2-3: Steps in the adoption journey.

- **Understand strategic intent**: Understand and evaluate the strategic intent of the business. Prepare for your cloud adoption journey by evaluating technology and understanding key adoption practices and the effects of organizational change.
- **Identify strategic opportunities**: Identify opportunities to accelerate digital transformation by acknowledging maturity levels across capabilities.
- **Ideate and prioritize**: Evaluate and prioritize ideas and recommendations; leverage attributes such as feasibility, impact, and cost to prioritize transformation activities.
- **Pilot and prove**: Test, prove, and pilot the recommendations; identify measurable outcomes, prove capability and validate with end users and against business-driven measurements.
- **Scale**: Scale while validating with end users; take iterative steps to validate approaches, confirm technical decisions, and begin adoption to cloud models at scale.
- **Define strategic outcomes**: Capitalize on proven successes, learn from feedback, and achieve benefits as you transform business processes.

This structured approach of discovery along important dimensions, together with a step-by-step adoption process with integrated decision-making, aligning with the user perspective and business objectives over the long term comprises our framework.

Given the long-term nature and effects of transformation, we recommend that you periodically take stock to gauge where your organization is versus where it needs to be. Revisiting the steps as outlined in Figure 2-3 is a practical approach for achieving continuous improvement.

We believe that if leaders of organizations apply this approach successfully, they will earn the right to act as their internal or external clients' undisputed transformation partners of choice in the future.

Ten Key Actions of the Framework

Digital transformation requires designing a strategic road map for sustained success. We believe that organizations must balance current and future technology needs in such a way that they understand the integrated set of decisions that need to be made over time, all aligned with the organization's technology adoption and digital transformation vision. The framework provides the decision-making approach to prioritize the capabilities that will have the largest effect on the business. The framework helps you adapt to your organization's changing needs along the way while maintaining a clear focus on strategic intent.

What we show next are ten key actions within the framework that we believe must be taken to ensure the types of alignment needed for successful outcomes.

1. Involve the right people

As cloud adoption and digital transformation have profound effects on an organization, you must engage the entire organization in the transformation. At the heart of any transformation is leadership at all levels of the organization, from the top down. Executive sponsorship that personally ensures that key decisions are made, defines what success looks like, and actively participates in the steps necessary for transformation to succeed is critical. We don't advocate micromanagement by the key executives of the organization; instead, we suggest that executives participate enough for the entire organization to see their personal stake in the cloud adoption and digital transformation initiatives.

Through our work, we have found that digital transformation projects with the right level of executive sponsorship (including key stakeholders from lines of business as well as technology) are more likely to succeed. We also find that when these leaders pay personal attention and help define the meaning of success, they create conditions allowing their teams to explore new ideas safely. This approach of fostering innovation shortens the time to success. Therefore, we suggest that transformation leaders follow a simple plan with the following steps:

a. Secure high-level executive sponsorship for the transformation.
b. Identify and engage key line-of-business, technology, and other key stakeholders.
c. Develop and execute a stakeholder communication plan for active engagement.

We have found this simple model to ensure that the cloud adoption and digital transformation program gains the level of visibility and buy-in that it requires. It also ensures that all the right perspectives are represented at the table and that communication and decision-making is clear. The communication plan should capture how much is communicated to the sponsors and stakeholders and how often it is communicated. The amount and frequency of communication will vary by organization and individual preferences. In our work with enterprises, we have found that using collaboration platforms such as Slack ensure team access to the most current and relevant content.

2. Achieve business and technology alignment

To be successful, you must bring multiple perspectives together to agree on your overall approach and primary deliverables. These deliverables include the economic case for cloud adoption and transformation, long-term adoption and transformation road maps, decisions on talent and culture, and key measures for success (both short- and long-term).

We have found that aligning on the approach and deliverables is necessary to ensure that the business stakeholders in your organization buy into the transformation program. Longer term, this includes securing the budget for the transformation initiatives once they are proposed. Two key lessons for us include developing a long-term roadmap even while delivering quick-wins and developing an economic case for cloud adoption and digital transformation that aligns the business view with the technology view.

The economic case for cloud adoption and digital transformation documents the reasons why the organization is undergoing the journey in the first place and lists the economic benefits that will be achieved. This case is required to persuade the business that cloud transformation and adoption is viable from a business perspective. One of the key lessons we have learned is that this case should neither be the first nor the last deliverable of this set that is produced. An economic case must be based on validated assumptions. Often, these assumptions — about staffing, productivity, trade-off of capital expenditure (Capex) to operational expenditure (Opex), and so on — cannot be validated until you have defined your road map for adoption and justified some of your assumptions through early pilots of small projects.

The cloud adoption and transformation road maps encourage the organization to envision the transformation over the long term. These road maps ensure that even when you undertake short-term efforts, that you identify, prioritize, and address topics that relate to the long-term goals of the transformation. The idea is not to complicate decision-making but to avoid missteps and create the basis for accelerated adoption and reduce the need for expensive rework.

3. Take a holistic approach across dimensions

Digital transformation requires a holistic approach across multiple dimensions, all which must be considered together in making decisions for successful outcomes. Each organization is unique, and the depth or breadth of discovery and decision-making will vary accordingly. Using the framework, you can build your own game plan in the way that works best for your organization. You might elect to prioritize one dimension of the framework over another, for example, or you might investigate one dimension to a deeper level of depth of inquiry versus another dimension. Composability, flexibility, and agility are key attributes of the framework. Although the framework is designed to be holistic, accounting for important dimensions of transformation, we commonly see our clients adapt it to suit their own needs. We define these three attributes in the following way:

- **Composability** means that in developing your game plan, you can assemble the elements of the framework that are of high priority to your organization. If the methodology dimension needs shoring up to achieve your goals, for example, you can focus on that dimension while understanding that you need all the other dimensions to complete the whole picture.

- Flexibility means that in these important dimensions, you only need to go to the level of depth required in your context to make decisions that move your plan forward.
- Agility means being ready to course-adjust to align with the needs of the business, learning from experimentation, building on the successes of the cloud adoption program, and evaluating and redirecting as needed.

The framework is designed to be tailored to your specific context while keeping in view the holistic and integrated set of decisions that together can propel your organization forward.

4. Assume an outside-in, client-centered approach

We believe that an outside-in, client-focused approach ensures alignment with business intent. In our work with enterprise clients, we apply IBM Design Thinking[1] techniques in order to get to the essence of what is important to the organization.

Design Thinking techniques allow us to articulate and prioritize business-needs statements that all stakeholders agree with. These approaches engage critical business stakeholders such that they own key milestones and play a crucial role in defining ultimate success. We should note that Design Thinking is not limited to user experience design; you can apply the techniques effectively to all parts of the transformation program. We cover design thinking extensively in Chapter 8.

5. Open the aperture to new possibilities

An enterprise is, by definition, complex, with unique values, people, cultures, behaviors, processes, and ways of doing things. Cloud adoption and digital transformation require enterprises to accept change, but that process touches all the existing parts of the enterprise. This leads you to several very difficult questions to address in the context of your organization:

- How can you create positive change within existing ways of doing things?
- How can you introduce new ideas safely, understanding that they can cause disruption?
- How do you enlist key stakeholders to make them part of the change?

Our approach to addressing all these questions begins by convening key stakeholders in what we refer to as an open ideation session. This approach allows us to introduce new ideas grounded in the practical experience of other enterprises.

Open ideation sessions are in-person sessions hosted by an expert in the field, with the objective being to explore a topic of interest to the organization or a dimension of the framework. The exploration provides specific guidance on the competencies that the enterprise needs to put in place to accelerate cloud adoption and digital transformation. A subject-matter expert (SME) leads the discussion but encourages free sharing and exchange of ideas among the participants. We have had IBM Distinguished Engineers, IBM Fellows, and industry experts lead open ideation sessions, following a simple discussion outline regardless of the specific topic of focus:

a. Introduce the topic within the enterprise and industry context.
b. Discuss key concepts related to the topic. The leader ensures that questions are addressed in a non-threatening way and that everyone understands that this is an opportunity to discuss the topic in a larger industry context, allowing ideas to come from many different sources.
c. Summarize key lessons and takeaways and assign owners of follow-ups.

We have found this simple format to be effective in providing structure yet encouraging discourse directly related to the topic of discussion. This format gives participants a grounded view of the topic provided by those who have lived and resolved challenges at close quarters. We understand that each organization is unique, with a unique value proposition. The open ideation session provides a safe, meaningful forum that opens the aperture, enabling new ideas and new foundations to be explored.

6. Show progress and quick wins

By definition and by design, digital transformation is a long-term endeavor. What success looks like can be quite different in the short term versus the long term. The key sponsors, stakeholders, and even end users can be vastly different between the start of a digital transformation project and its conclusion.

Given the low barrier to entry into new or adjacent market spaces, your future core markets may be radically different from the markets your organization serves today. Over three to five years, the same may be true of the services you offer.

Considering this changing landscape and the need to sustain sponsorship, you must continuously align to business and markets requirements. How do you continue to generate momentum, enabling the virtuous circle that is needed for long-term success?

We have found that you must build into the transformation program a way to show progress through quick wins while keeping the long view in focus. This helps showcase and sustain the overall cloud adoption and digital transformation program. We have been able to show organizations how to spotlight these quick wins, driving real value in the short term while squarely aligning with each organization's long-term objectives and definition of success, creating a virtuous circle that can sustain success in the long term. Here are two examples of quick wins that we have spotlighted with our clients:

- At our global multinational banking client, a workload and data classification decision-making plan was established to drive cloud application modernization. For application workloads and data deemed to have good affinity with a private cloud environment, we were able to complete this analysis on a compressed schedule. As a result, the client was ready to implement the move to the cloud in record time: 2 months, versus the original 6- to 12-month estimate.
- At our global airline client, the customer transformation champion identified a small promotional application that was outside the original scope of the transformation but that had high executive visibility. The challenge was that the scheduled promotion was about to start, but the application had not even been implemented. We were able to quickly bring resources, best practices, and tooling to bear to build the application. As a result, the team moved the application from concept to production within two months, gaining credibility and good will with the technology and business leaders alike. This translated into more applications for this business unit being added to the transformation scope.

We have found that periodically showcasing such quick wins in what we refer to as a *spotlight* demonstrates success in a tangible way. The spotlight provides the program platform to showcase short-term cloud adoption success to support the long-term transformation journey. The spotlight should be included in the stakeholder communication plan to document evidence of progress.

7. Collaborate actively

Collaboration and co-creation are crucial to the success of any cloud adoption and digital transformation program. Experience has proved to us that when participants from organizations are directly involved in shaping their own destiny, they take a personal stake in the success of the overall project. We recommend co-located innovation and co-creation spaces where SMEs and clients work together collaboratively, face to face. We have found that taking advantage of such face-to-face time in inviting spaces can encourage creativity. Therefore, we encourage the use of spaces such as IBM Design Studios and IBM Cloud Garages, as well as other spaces that can spur and support the creative process.

Through our work, we have found the following techniques to be effective:

- Pair experts from IBM with client experts for the same dimension or topic area. We discuss this topic in more depth in Chapter 8 on Methodology.
- Include line-of-business SMEs in the technical discussions. We also discuss this topic in Chapter 8 on Methodology.
- Have developers work closely with operations SMEs to address adjacent DevOps topics. This topic is a main subject of Chapter 9 on Service Management and Operations.

We have found that when key stakeholders spend time in person collaborating on some of the most challenging topics that enterprises face, the outcomes can be significant — even breathtaking.

8. Balance sustained and disruptive innovation

You must strike a balance between sustained innovation and disruptive innovation to keep pace with market forces and business priorities. The framework enables decision-making so that you can understand how both the current state and the future state align with business intent.

Our experience is that you must clearly outline criteria along all the key dimensions in order to enable decision-making for the types of trade-offs that need to be made. Where your organization sits on the spectrum between sustained innovation and disruptive innovation and which decisions need to be made depend on factors specific to your organization and your priorities. What your organization must do is determine a set of to-be states to be phased in over time. Each to-be state should provide incremental value at each new level of maturity.

To get to that set of to-be states, you first perform assessments of your maturity along each dimension. You may then want to use tools such as spider charts and heat maps to identify what the most critical items are along each dimension. Then you must set up a step-by-step plan that includes findings and recommendations to get to each new desired state over time.

Please note that your placement on that spectrum is merely a point-in-time evaluation. As with a long view on digital transformation, your enterprise's disposition is likely to change over time, so we recommend periodic reevaluation.

9. Establish success criteria

You need to establish clear success criteria and deliverables for each of the framework's key dimensions, which includes getting sign-off by key stakeholders and participating collaborators. Doing so means that everyone participating in the cloud adoption and digital transformation program has a stake in the successful implementation of the recommendations.

Clear deliverables and sign-off on these deliverables ensure accountability and proper care in the production of these artifacts. In our work, we have seen that clearly defining the deliverables/sign-off policies encourages diligence and minimizes unnecessary, redundant work. This way, the co-creating participants and teams know that they themselves must do high-quality work to develop the agreed-on deliverables.

10. Account for a multicloud hybrid model

Most enterprises have a multivendor and multicloud hybrid environment, a fact that continues to be borne out in our global work with enterprise clients. The trends continue to point to multicloud hybrid environments: on-premises private clouds, connected to off-premises services forming islands of value with federation and connectivity. In many of these hybrid environments, we also observe multiple-vendor solutions and services.

Enterprise cloud environments often include both open-source and proprietary vendor capabilities. Whether these multicloud environments are arrived at accidentally through shadow IT or through a deliberate process of multi-vendor cloud adoption, the framework recognizes this reality and assumes a vendor-agnostic approach. We discuss this multicloud future in more depth in Chapter 7 on Emerging Technology Spaces.

Summary

The framework builds on an enterprise's existing investments while transforming to new foundations, giving you an advantage over time. You can leverage the framework to bring together key technology and business stakeholders within your organization to develop recommendations and make the key decisions that need to be made along the digital transformation journey:

- **Think and Envision the Transformation** to establish the strategic intent of the transformation
- **Balance the Transformation** to decide what works best for the enterprise
- **Thrive on New Foundations** to realize the strategic outcomes at scale and over a sustained period of time

We designed the framework to provide a structure for effective decision-making to help you prioritize the capabilities that will have the largest effect to the business, adapting to your organization's changing needs along the way, with a clear focus on strategic intent and key enablers.

3 Strategy

A vision without a strategy remains an illusion.

—Lee Bolman

A cloud strategy helps define the outcomes a business seeks. It also lays out how you are going to get there. Having a cloud strategy enables an organization to connect adoption elements, understand dependencies, and ultimately help speedy execution, with fewer delays.

It may be a surprise that after so many years, cloud adoption remains a top of mind challenge for many organizations. While the value of cloud is well understood, and investments are funneled to make progress towards a cloud-based transformation, our experience highlights that only a small percentage of enterprises had a documented cloud adoption strategy.

As organizations look to accelerate adoption, applying best practice becomes critical to the success of developing a cloud strategy. A successful cloud strategy would not slow down an organization, nor would it stifle agility, autonomy or flexibility of the IT or business departments. It would instead increase understanding of how decisions on cloud can impact the business services, departments, and individuals and unite the organization behind a unified vision and a roadmap. It is a case of: *sometimes you have to slow down to speed up.*

The goal is to develop a strategy that is executable. That strategy should translate vision into practical roadmaps that are broad, prescriptive, actionable, and most critically, flexible. Flexibility in execution is required in the fast-changing and dynamic world of cloud.

In this chapter, we explore four key questions, often leveraged to help frame and shape a cloud strategy. For each, we walk through a tried and tested structure that helps us formulate the necessary understanding and direction to take.

What Does a Cloud Strategy Mean for the CIO?

For the past few years, chief executive officers (CEOs) have identified technology as the number-one factor they see affecting the success of their businesses.[1]

For them, technology is not just part of the infrastructure needed to implement a business strategy; it's what makes entirely new strategies possible. Without technology in place in a meaningful way to spark continual innovation, they fear being left behind. As a result, chief information officers (CIOs) foresee a major shift in their own priorities as they evolve from service provider to strategic enabler.

Ninety percent of business and technology executives are including cloud computing in their current or three-year plans.[2] That should be no surprise, given the emergence of the cloud as a catalyst for continual innovation across both business and IT. The cloud is rapidly evolving. What started as a scoped play to reduce infrastructure capital expenses and in-house administration costs has evolved to be a broad catalyst for reinventing consumer interactions, entire businesses, and even established industries. *Leaders are using the cloud as a crucible to forge business transformation.* Figure 3-1 illustrates how several industry trends such as the Internet of things (IOT), Augmented Reality (AR), Artificial Intelligence (AI), and social media are driving customers towards cloud. Such transformations don't happen overnight. Seasoned leaders understand this process will be a journey requiring a strategy and a plan.

As leaders initiate their cloud transformation initiative, the natural first step is formulating a targeted strategy (in the context of their organization and industry) for tackling this journey.

What Do We Really Mean by "Strategy"?

Strategy is that which enables alignment between vision and execution. Simply put, strategy is a set of integrated decisions that guide you in aligning with a defined vision relative to the competition.

A strategy enables you to decide what markets to participate in, how to participate, and what capabilities you must have to be successful (including technology, talent, and skill). It also tells you what management systems need to be in place to be effective, the time frame in which they need to be executed to be relevant, and how you know that you are succeeding. Any strategy should, of course, be refined over time in a virtuous feedback loop as it is executed.

Our experience is that a strategy is not a single manifesto, but an overarching direction and plan that can be forked to address execution needs. Strategy execution needs to be localized to fit different markets. That is, the way you deploy and localize execution of strategy in different markets will differ for your specific markets and considerations.

Our belief is that for organizations to excel, to serve their markets and customers exceptionally, and to return shareholder value, you must precisely understand who you serve, what you build, how you earn a profit, what capability you need, and how you engage to deliver value. This understanding is a prerequisite to being a trusted, essential part of delivering value to your organization. CIOs, chief strategy officers (CSOs), and other leaders and catalysts for digital transformation must gain visibility and credibility by showing alignment of strategic intent and outcomes through real execution.

Strategy, especially in the enterprise context, can get quite involved and complicated. For our purposes in getting to the essence of how strategy and strategy execution manifest, and for brevity, we will keep our descriptions simple.

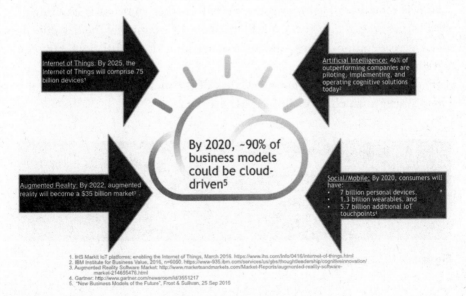

Figure 3-1: Cloud as a crucible for business transformation.

Developing a Cloud Strategy

When it comes to developing a cloud strategy, CIOs, CSOs, and leaders involved in setting business direction repeatedly ask us:

- What are the complete dimensions of a cloud strategy?
- What key considerations should a cloud strategy address?
- What prescriptive steps are required to develop a cloud strategy?
- What proven approaches and methods best suit my organization?

Answering these questions starts with understanding the need for clear objectives, with these objectives supported by a strategy that guides the transformation. We have learned from the many engagements we have completed that for the CIO, *a cloud strategy is a must*. A cloud strategy articulates the strategic business intent and expected outcomes. For the CIO, a strategy acts as a *guide* for enabling the larger digital transformation and as a *guard* against fragmented, endless experimentation with no systemic effect.

If the strategy is executed correctly, it leads to meaningful, self-evident value to the business. Note that the cloud strategy by itself is a necessary but insufficient condition for success. That strategy must be actionable for the value to be realized.

In the remainder of this chapter, we will further your understanding of cloud strategy and answer the questions above by examining the key dimensions, considerations, steps, and approaches for a successful cloud strategy development and execution plan.

Figure 3-2 illustrates a summary view of the important dimensions of a cloud strategy, which we examined in Chapter 2.

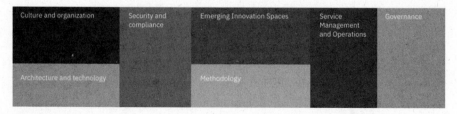

Figure 3-2: Summary view of Important dimensions of cloud strategy.

Figure 3-3 illustrates the processes of developing a cloud strategy; that includes the key topics to consider, the steps involved, and a prescriptive approach guide. You must consider the key technological and organizational considerations needed to influence your cloud strategy. You must also determine a set of decisions along different dimensions that describe the aspects that you must consider in your cloud strategy; this is where you have to determine whether your organization needs to change and what aspects of it must change. Finally, once you have decided what you need to do, you can follow our prescriptive set of steps to develop an executable cloud strategy. Of course, what you learn in following the prescriptive steps will force you to re-evaluate your previous decisions along the cloud dimensions. Iteration and stepwise refinement are expected parts of the overall strategy formulation process. We will begin by examining the dimensions of the cloud strategy you will formulate.

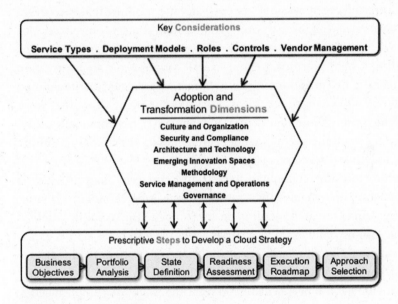

Figure 3-3: Developing a cloud strategy.

What Are the Complete Dimensions of a Cloud Strategy?

Usually, an organization that is looking to get a solid start or a good handle on its cloud strategy already has several cloud-related initiatives live or in the pipeline. We often see lines of businesses experimenting in a "shadow IT" mode or a sales group already using cloud solutions from cloud-based vendors such as Salesforce.com. Observing all the groups and departments of an organization pursuing their own agendas, the CIO and often the chief financial officer (CFO) usually intervene to formalize an enterprise wide unified cloud strategy. Given the cross-organization interest, completeness of thought becomes critical in involvement and buy-in from the various stakeholders.

In Chapter 2, we introduced the adoption and transformation framework, noting the thought process that went into developing the framework as a comprehensive representation of the enterprise adoption journey. When it comes to structuring the cloud strategy, those dimensions provide the guidepost for outlining strategy decisions and most importantly, execution.

For completeness, a cloud strategy needs to be scoped to the following dimensions:

- **Culture and organization:** Proactively develop a culture that encourages innovation and aligns with your organization's strategic objectives. This dimension is probably the most challenging for most organizations, and getting it right is critical to your overall adoption and transformation outcomes. Organizational structures that encourage experimentation and risk allow you to test ideas quickly, supporting those that work and discarding those that do not in a blame-free environment. Always keep focus on the overall business outcomes as you develop a culture to catalyze and accelerate innovation.

- **Architecture and technology:** Architecture and technology provide the core fabric that enables the transformation. A successful cloud strategy grounds the architecture and technology dimension in practical return-on-investment (ROI) analysis while allowing rapid market experimentation. This dimension is where most organizations tend to leap to first. Our experience strongly cautions that careful consideration is necessary to establish overall clarity on what you want to accomplish before jumping directly into technology choices. Getting this dimension right is significant in minimizing costly rework in the future. Understanding the different types of cloud services, applications, the nature of data, and affinity for the types of target cloud architectures and technologies that must support your cloud services, applications, and data is critical to driving overall adoption and transformation success.

- **Security and compliance:** Proactively developing and embedding the right security and compliance policies and capabilities is important. Understanding the effect of the regulatory environment enables you to formulate the right compliance and security posture for your organization while supporting the innovation agenda. For example, your cloud adoption and transformation strategy must account for potentially refactoring applications and data storage approaches in order to meet Personally Identifiable Information (PII) requirements.

- **Methodology:** If speed and agility are key outcomes, methodology is the dimension that focuses on the mechanisms for enabling these outcomes. It is worth noting that in our experience, this dimension needs to be addressed for all prioritized delivery targets. The methodology dimension is not exclusive to cloud-native applications.

- **Emerging Innovation Spaces:** Understanding new and emerging innovation spaces, quickly experimenting with these innovations, conducting user assures that you can take advantage of these innovations quickly ahead of the marketing. Inculcating a culture that encourages the fostering and application of new ideas means that you always have a pulse on technology. The application of these new technologies to real user and business need, however, yields innovation of direct relevance to the business.

- **Service management and operations:** Like the methodology dimension, an approach to transforming operations is critical in yielding speed and efficiency. The service management and operations dimension would consider a phasing-in of critical IT infrastructure library (ITIL) processes, refined to incorporate the cloud operating model. Tools, skills, vendor relationships, service levels, and in-house investments to upgrade the operational model all need to be thought through as part of this dimension.

- **Governance:** Governance provides the *decision rights framework* and the policies that inform management practices and execution. Clarify and visibility in responsibility and accountability matrices can engender transparent, effective decision-making within your organization. Your governance model should align with your overall cloud strategy and the organization that is affected by or that needs to execute the strategy. You should actively and continuously evaluate the governance framework definition and the shifts required from traditional structures, and from centralized control to more flexible governance approaches that are supportive of an agile culture.

What Key Considerations Should a Cloud Strategy Address?

Creating a cloud computing strategy will establish a road map to achieve your vision for a transformed enterprise. First, your organization must coalesce around a common scope and perspective for the cloud. Consider these two perspectives:

- Cloud, the industrialization of delivery for IT services, is a new consumption and delivery model inspired by consumer Internet services. This model is enabled by service automation, virtualization, and standardization via self-service, economies of scale, flexible pricing models, and workload-based IT resource provisioning.
- Cloud computing is a model for enabling convenient, on-demand network access to a shared pool of configurable resources (such as networks, servers, storage, applications, and services) that can be rapidly provisioned and released with reduced management effort or service-provider interaction.

Each of these definitions reflects an accurate view of cloud through a different lens. Your organization's definition of cloud depends on its unique perspective, and the sheer variability of cloud and the value it offers create vast opportunities for a customized view.

Given these broad parameters, your organization must determine how cloud's flexibility can serve your business and strategic objectives. Your challenge is to determine, in the context of the dimensions we discussed earlier, the definition of cloud that is relevant for you. You should closely address the following key considerations:

- Service types
- Deployment models
- Roles
- Controls
- Vendor relationships

These considerations may seem to be wide-ranging, but remember: *Strategy is that which enables alignment between vision and execution.* Through our client engagements, we have learned that our clients must be able to account for these considerations to have a solid baseline of clarity for any strategy-related execution plan. Next, we will examine each consideration in turn.

Service types

You should already be familiar with the foundational concepts of the cloud, often described as Infrastructure as a Service (IaaS), Platform as a Service (PaaS), and Software as a Service (SaaS). These concepts remain valid and important in establishing a common understanding of the general service types.

Since the early inception of the cloud and the National Institute of Standards and Technology (NIST) definition from 2011 (see Chapter 1), the industry and clients with which we work closely have continued to evolve to a more expansive view of service types. We see increased affinity between the IaaS and the PaaS layer, for example; the utility and popularity of containerization have introduced what is commonly referred to a Containers as a Service (CaaS); advancements in new serverless architectures have brought forward Functions as a Service (FaaS) as another variant. Within the construct of a cloud strategy, these concepts can be combined and considered to be part of the Cloud Foundation layer as shown in Figure 3-4.

The next set of layers decomposes SaaS into three tiers, called Data, Cognitive, and Solutions:

- **Data:** We see the emergence of Data as a Service (DaaS). As in networking, storage, and compute capabilities are a necessary core of any IaaS; capabilities such as ingestion, cleansing, masking, deployment, and governance are for any DaaS. From a strategy-development perspective, the scope needs to define what the data sources are and how data is classified and treated (and at what granularity).
- **Cognitive:** Virtually every organization we are engaged with is thinking through ways of differentiating its business by using cognitive capabilities such as artificial intelligence (AI), machine learning, deep learning, and predictive analytics. From a strategy-development perspective, the scope needs to link to the organization's cognitive strategy and define the critical set of services that will be part of the baseline and the differentiated value delivered.
- **Solutions:** Solutions are the most common type of SaaS and are mostly well-formed units of value or compositions of such. Examples include complete human-resources and customer-relationship-management solutions.

We see clear solution spaces — sales opportunity management, client management, employee management, and many more — that are industry-driven. From a strategy-development perspective, the scope needs to identify not only the solutions to be consumed, but also the critical integration elements and linkages between those solutions and the rest of the *composite business applications*.

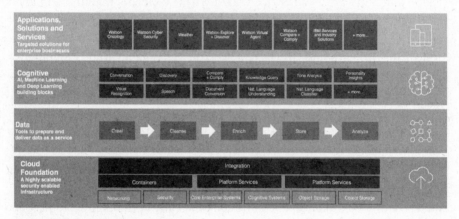

Figure 3-4: Cloud service types.

Deployment models

Like service types, the broad choices of deployment model should be familiar. Public and private in the broadest terms form the basis of more granular choices such as shared public, dedicated public, hosted private, managed private, and on-premises private. These different deployment models are illustrated in Figure 3-5.

The keys from a strategy-development perspective are to define the best fit based on business and technical considerations and to recognize the need for a multicloud approach that provides the most choice to your enterprise. Our experience bears out the prudence of this approach, which allows you to take advantage of different cloud deployment models and the services offered by those models. We cover this set of decisions later in Chapter 3 as we explore controls and workloads.

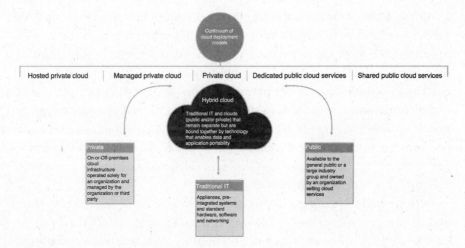

Figure 3-5: Cloud deployment models.

Roles

Other important decisions depend upon which role or roles your organization assumes. It could take on one or more of three possibilities; consumer, integrator, or provider:

Consumer

If you are a *consumer* of a public cloud, you are most likely to work with an external cloud service provider. In the case that you are a consumer of a public cloud, your organization will need to establish an *integrator* role to manage the interaction, expectations, performance, contracts, and other factors that are part of your relationship with the provider.

Often, the private-versus-public cloud question is not a mutually exclusive one; you should view it through the prism of what works best for your organization and the purposes for which your business requires specific deployment models. We have seen organizations opt for both in a *hybrid cloud* model.

Although the advantages are clear (given that such an environment enables access, use, and/or deployment of services and applications in the best fit for purpose environments), these environments can result in sourcing and management challenges, given the complexity that they introduce. These new challenges include (but are not limited to) data locality; workload placement and mobility; integration of systems, including industrialized core or legacy systems; visibility, providing a clear line of sight into overall system health (including availability); performance and cross-cloud security; and service and software licensing portability. These considerations are important in fully realizing the value of the hybrid model.

In the remaining chapters in this book, we examine solutions, approaches, and techniques that we have worked on with clients to consider these important topics and to realize this full potential of cloud adoption and digital transformation.

Integrator

We see in our work that the *integrator* role is of ever-increasing importance because it holds accountability for cloud services provided by an external party (or parties.) This role requires technology and business acumen to clearly translate business and technical requirements into integration with service providers. In effect, the integrator becomes your organization's liaison to all third-party providers and the interface that manages relationships, expectations, and outcomes in these interactions on behalf of your organization. Internal IT or an outsourcing partner can play the integrator role on behalf of your entire organization.

Provider

If you have ownership or custody of the assets needed to deliver cloud services to the consumer, and if those assets could be different based on the service layer, you play the role of the cloud service *provider*. As the provider, you can offer private or shared cloud services to your own internal organizational users or provide services to an entity outside your organization. A service provider plays a critical role in a hybrid computing model.

Must you define your organization strictly in terms of these roles? Not necessarily. In fact, a *hybrid enterprise* means that you will likely need to assume more than one role: *consumer, integrator, and provider.* Understanding that fact up front will have significant positive downstream effects as you build execution plans that support your overall cloud strategy. See Figure 3-6.

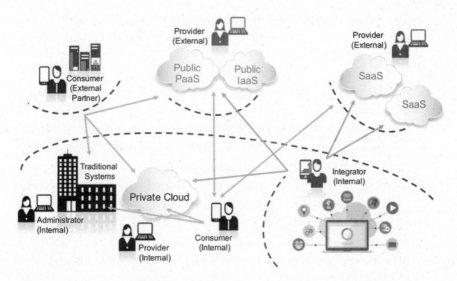

Figure 3-6: Hybrid enterprise.

Controls

Controls apply to governance, organization design, security and compliance, and operations. They involve oversight by your organization of things such as policies, procedures, and standards for IT service acquisition, as well as the design, implementation, testing, use, and monitoring of deployed services.

Compliance and risk management are governance processes that have always been critical to traditional IT systems, and they are equally vital to the cloud. What is different for cloud is an expanded set of considerations. Given that cloud services are often sourced outside the IT organization, lack of controls can put the organization in jeopardy, creating privacy, security, compliance, business continuity, legal, and even reputational risks. Cloud silos or clutter often result when governance is not clearly established.

Robust cloud governance should be part of your cloud computing strategy. Cloud governance includes

- Identifying stakeholders and establishing decision-rights frameworks for all who participate in the cloud ecosystem, including service procurement
- Developing cloud decision-making processes for critical processes
- Codifying and enforcing policies to manage cloud services, environment, and providers

Finally, a cloud strategy requires design and operational capabilities that many organizations lack. The list of requirements is long and often challenging, including:

- A post-shared-services governance model that imbibes the basic tenets of the cloud
- Sourcing and procurement processes that engage in just-in-time sourcing
- Integrated event, change, release, capacity, and service-level management that provide visibility, automation, and control
- Metering, rating, billing, and cloud service subscription management that support transparency and accountability
- Offering management that recognizes your users' needs and responds to those needs quickly
- Standardized services and the platforms that support them to help you industrialize service delivery and service support
- A critical mass of resources that can be pooled to justify the investment and achieve required economies of scale
- Software licensing agreements tailored to a cloud consumption model
- An integrated and consistent view of the industrialized core combined with the new programming models, leveraging techniques, and application programming interfaces (APIs) to amplify value to your organization and beyond

These considerations give you the flexibility to fulfill specific and even unique IT requirements and to stand differentiated in the market as you support your strategic intent. You need, however, a thoughtful approach to assembling an optimum portfolio of IT-delivered services with the associated flexibility and controls in place. You should be able to apply the appropriate level of structure to ensure compliance, achievement of service-level agreements (SLAs), and effective security without creating overbearing processes and complexity, for example. You can achieve these benefits by balancing flexibility with structure. You should view cloud computing as an *expansion* of more structured, traditional IT delivery alternatives instead of a *replacement* for them.

In summary, as you develop a governance execution plan to support existing services (part of the industrialized core) and to develop and acquire new services, you need to evaluate this range of services from a fresh perspective that embraces a range of delivery possibilities. Solutions that do not fit into a well-developed overall enterprise cloud model can create an expensive and incompatible portfolio of IT services — the opposite of the cloud objective of architecting solutions from standard components, integrated for flexibility and delivered in an optimum way.

Vendor relationships

Although you may want to approach a new transformative initiative without assuming burdens, you must consider existing and future strategic vendor relationships to be part of the initiative. In our experience, organizations forge the most successful cloud strategies by involving one or more strategic vendors as partners.

When selecting vendors for this partnership, you must account for established contracts, the ability of a vendor to execute, alignment on direction and goals, and the vendor's maturity with cloud technologies. You must also consider the vendor's ability to execute where you need them to, be it on their specialty area of expertise or on their capability in specific geographies. It is also important to define the roles that ecosystem partners can play in supporting your strategic intent. The focus is often on the technology provider but should extend to vendors that can effectively support transformation, design, training, co-creation, and ongoing management opportunities.

As in all competitive markets, vendors in the cloud space are vying for lead positions and exclusivity with existing clients or prospects. The reality, however, is that enterprises almost certainly need to develop a cloud ecosystem. Factors discussed earlier, such as multicloud, hybrid cloud requirements, and avoiding lock-in drive an enterprise toward the notion of an ecosystem of providers with a rich menu of services governed by the requirements of the enterprise. Even if an enterprise opts for an exclusive off-premises policy, it is still likely to involve integration and management across IaaS, PaaS, and SaaS providers. Therefore, the ecosystem is inevitable in most cases.

Here are some additional considerations to bear in mind in formulating your cloud strategy.

Seek meaningful partnerships

We have seldom observed an enterprise successfully going it alone, as they run the risk of shifting from their core mission, diverting valuable time and resources into developing capability themselves. We recommend that you seek meaningful partnerships across the life cycle: from strategy to design to execution and maintenance. Viewed objectively, a well-articulated cloud strategy creates an opportunity to define the relationships between your organization and vendors, as well as the relationships among vendors — especially critical in the inevitable hybrid, multicloud enterprise.

Take advantage of your existing IT estates

Most organizations have invested in enterprise application estates. Many of your existing partners are in turn investing heavily in bringing the cloud experience to these offerings, either through shift-to-cloud models or tried-and-tested integration and refactoring techniques.

IBM is an example, providing offerings for enterprise middleware and data stack (WebSphere Application Server, databases, MQ, and others) as containerized solutions (for rapid consumption and scale) or managed services. SAP is another example of a partner offering a suite of solutions (including those related to human resources, human capital management, and SAP HANA) in the cloud.

In such environments, application, platform, and management layers integrate seamlessly, resulting in significantly lower migration burden for the enterprise. Our observation in these cases is that leveraging existing partnerships can be significantly advantageous.

Continually learn and evaluate

Many early adopters of cloud technologies invest in specific vendors or vendor solutions. Often, enterprises have made such a start with public cloud services (Amazon Web Services, IBM, Microsoft Azure, Google, and so on) or private cloud environments (adopting a build-your-own-cloud approach by using OpenStack, VMware, Red Hat, and other solutions).

Depending on the success of these programs, many organizations are inclined to continue along the same path, particularly when they have invested in skills or talent aligned with these specific platforms.

Our recommendation is not to default to a conclusion but to continually evaluate and seek alignment with strategic outcomes. We have observed that as technologies have matured and enterprises have gained knowledge and experience with their early forays into the cloud, rethinking and recalibration have occurred. Build-your-own-cloud initiatives can prove to be quite costly over the long term, and they tend to deviate from being open as originally intended, becoming quite customized, unwieldy, and difficult to support.

Organizations that pause, step back, and measure their current position against where they need to be are in many cases getting back to basics: Are they still on the right path, given their strategic intent? What actions do they need to take to accelerate their cloud adoption and transformation journey? What investment is needed to fulfill these objectives and achieve full potential? It is important to reevaluate these questions to help determine any required adjustments.

Seek standardized solutions for commoditize capability

Our observation is that early decisions that led to highly customized, unwieldy systems are giving way to standardized vendor solutions, allowing valuable enterprise resources to focus on higher-value function. This change is occurring in both the private and public cloud models, as new hybrid architectures become the norm in multicloud environments, consistent with enterprise requirements for geographic presence, performance, and avoidance of vendor lock-in.

Consider specialized services for differentiated value

You need to consider your organization's desired and expected use of specialized cloud services. If the enterprise needs to leverage certain cloud services (such as cognitive intelligence, AI, Big Data, or Internet of Things [IoT] services), a selection of best-of-breed vendors based on your organization's requirements makes sense. The same is true for industry and function packaged solutions.

Reduce complexity and scale what works across the organization

You need to think broadly about the digital transformation across the enterprise and not focus only on the architecture and technology dimension. What works in the small scale may not work at the level of your entire enterprise. Many vendors may provide best-of-breed point capabilities but lack scale, depth, or understanding of global enterprise transformation. If your organization intends the cloud initiative to be a transformation of how you work and deliver value aligned with your strategic intent, we strongly recommend selecting a vendor that can help with all the adoption and transformation dimensions we discussed earlier.

What Prescriptive Steps Are Required to Develop a Cloud Strategy?

Much of the early use of cloud was pioneered by individual line-of-business and application teams within larger companies, often outside the budgets and controls of the CIO. Now, however, IT teams and broader supporting units within an enterprise must develop strategies that enable and support cloud use across the enterprise.

To deliver on new cloud imperatives, CIOs across industries are moving rapidly to reexamine and redesign their entire approach. Our formula for developing cloud strategies has been tried and tested in transformations across thousands of enterprises. This simple formula includes six actions aligned to the adoption and transformation dimensions that take into account the considerations we discussed earlier. The six steps are

1. Define business objectives and constraints.
2. Complete analysis of your workload portfolio.
3. Envision your future state and analyze your current state.
4. Assess your organization's readiness.
5. Build an execution framework with defined strategic milestones.
6. Define proven approaches best suited to your organization.

Next, we explore each of those steps in turn.

Step 1: Define business objectives and constraints

Strategy starts with deciding how to carry out the organization's vision. Deciding what you want to accomplish with cloud computing is just as critical as executing that decision to achieve the intended outcomes. You must start with the end in mind by considering the possible list of outcomes. The choices you make here determine where you want to go, what the value of the digital transformation will be, and what your priorities for the organization will be. There are many desired and potential outcomes. Here are some of the most common:

■ **Competitiveness:** We define *competitiveness* as the ability to respond to a market opportunity with unique value, often leveraging design, technology, and operational excellence as differentiators. Competitiveness must incorporate the ability to respond across business lines and in an integrated fashion.

- **Agility**: *Agility* is the ability to pivot, proactively react, and respond to changing business realities in a rapid, sustained fashion. All parts of the organization (business, IT, and supporting functions) must be able to react at (or at nearly) the same pace for the organization to respond in an agile way.

- **Speed**: *Speed* is the ability to innovate and change faster than your current pace and show results quickly. Speed presumes the ability to do so through more efficient execution across the value stream.

- **Cost savings**: *Cost savings* is the ability to take advantage of the collective resource pool, which ultimately means saving money. It requires that you create efficiencies across the value stream without shifting the burden from one side to another. For example, swapping capital expenditure (CapEx) savings for operating expenditure (OpEx) costs shifts the burden and does not ultimately save money. Eliminating redundant infrastructure or reducing development costs through eliminating unneeded software licenses will save costs, however.

- **Focus**: *Focus* is the ability to pay attention to your core business to the exclusion of extraneous activities. Service delivery and management may be a responsibility that you want to shed, for example. Focusing on your core business allows you to more precisely determine where to invest time and money, but you must also understand and maintain control of your end-to-end costs, ensuring that the savings are real, not illusory.

Identifying constraints against these objectives is as critical as highlighting the goals. Constraints can range from commonly understood restrictions on privacy, locality, security, or data compliance or can be as subtle as existing agreements and timelines. Here is an example of a business objective that needs to be called out as a restriction: Some organizations have quickly evolved to an API economy with defined SLAs that are both end-user and business-to-business critical. Our experience with cloud strategy, adoption, and transformation projects often highlights a gap in organizational understanding of these restrictions. That is not surprising, given the silo responsibilities that are common in most traditional business/IT environments. When it comes to cloud strategy, there is an opportunity to break down silos and gain clarity on what is needed for your strategy to be viable.

Step 2: Complete analysis of your workload portfolio

The next step in formulating a strategy is analyzing your portfolio of workloads (existing as well as planned, applications as well as data) to determine their final disposition.

From a strategy-development perspective, the key is determining which workloads are best suited to which types of cloud deployment model or even to the cloud in the first place. You need to evaluate which workloads (meaning a capability or combination of IT capabilities and services that can make up an application) to start afresh with refactor, enhance, or migrate.

A useful practice is to decompose your enterprise workloads into an affinity/readiness matrix. These matrices divide up the set of enterprise workloads into business units and functional areas within the business unit. The heat map diagram is color-coded to indicate the readiness (in terms of ready to move to the cloud, may be made ready, or not ready) of each workload within the business unit and functional area. A close examination of an example portfolio of banking applications illustrates the point. See Figure 3-7 for an example:

We take a three-step, two-level approach to assessing these applications. The first level is to determine your objectives in the areas of Business Value, Risk Exposure, and Technology Fit. Once you have decided upon those, you then determine the individual criteria by which applications will be assessed.

When you first assess the feasibility of the cloud for your workloads, your initial questions should revolve around business value:

- What is the real cost benefit of moving those workloads to the cloud?
- How will that migration affect the ecosystem?

Next you should consider the risk profile of moving this application:

- What existing (known) risks could this move exacerbate?
- Are there new categories of risk that organization might be exposed to?

Finally, you should consider the technical aspects of the migration:

- Is the application designed in a way that is compatible with cloud services?
- Is it technically feasible to "disentangle" the application from others?

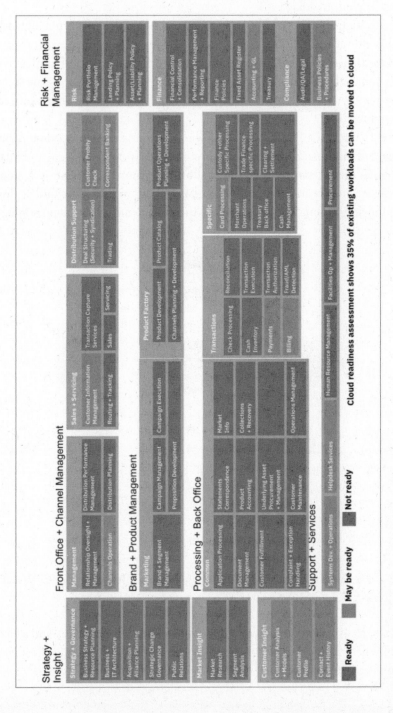

Figure 3-7: Workload and data assessment.

We discuss a more in-depth set of questions and considerations for workload assessment in Chapter 5.

Even though cloud environments exhibit immense flexibility, not all workloads are suitable for cloud deployment, so you also want to explore new workloads that are enabled by the cloud. Such workloads (such as high-volume, low-cost analytics; collaborative business networks; and industry-scale smart applications) can quickly create business value and enhance innovation for your organization.

From a strategy-development point of view, selecting the workloads and data to target and understanding their cloud suitability from a technical and business benefit prospective are key, and as shown in Figure 3-8. In our judgment, this assessment of workload and data, and matching to the right cloud deployment model represent one of the most critical elements of any cloud strategy.

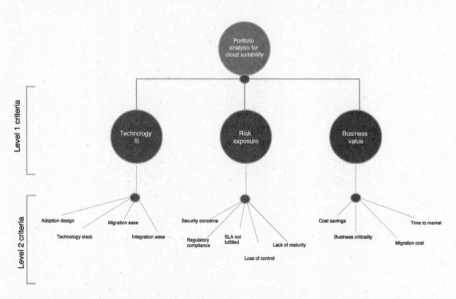

Figure 3-8: Workload and data disposition.

Step 3: Envision your future state and analyze your current state

When the goals have been agreed to, the constraints are validated, and a clear view of where to start is established, the next logical step in building your strategy is producing a gap analysis of your current and future states.

Envisioning the future state is best achieved by thinking about the value delivered to your client. The single most significant benefit of taking this approach is the ability to unify stakeholders around the common goal of the consumer experience. To shape that view, we recommend leveraging IBM Design Thinking, a framework that helps teams understand and deliver great user outcomes at the speed and scale of the enterprise. IBM Design Thinking begins with a focus on user outcomes, a multidisciplinary team, and a set of practices that allow for continuous reinvention of the end experience. The future state can delve into function-specific goals, such as cost of ownership, time to value, and business alignment. To articulate the combination of such views, use client-focused value statements (such as the ability to respond to a prioritized client's application function-change request in less than two weeks).

In understanding the current state, it is best to take a holistic view of any transformation and to do so in a cross-functional manner making sure to include important business and technology perspectives. That means less emphasis in the early stages on the function-specific constraints (an organization takes more than 12 hours to request a server, for example) and more focus on cross-functional constraints (from user story to delivery, an organization averages 16 weeks of effort, for example). The latter example starts to expose key gaps across functional areas, from design to development to operations and beyond.

By examining an end-to-end process flow, you can establish a link between the two states. One approach that we often leverage and recommend is value-stream mapping. According to *Goldratt's Theory of Constraints* any improvement made in a process before or after a process bottleneck only makes the overall process less efficient.

When you pause and think about that statement, you see that it makes sense. Do you know where your bottlenecks are, however? You may be familiar with a few that surface frequently. On average, it may take six build reruns before a stable build is produced, for example. Is that bottleneck the biggest one in the entire flow, or could it be something else? Even if it takes six reruns for a build to complete, does it matter if it takes a full two weeks to deploy the code into production?

Value stream mapping is a *Six Sigma* lean enterprise technique used to document, analyze, and improve the flow of information or materials required to produce a product or service for a customer. As related to cloud environments, value stream mapping can help identify bottlenecks in processes, and therefore point to improvements — which become critical success factors. See Figure 3-9 for an example of a value stream map.

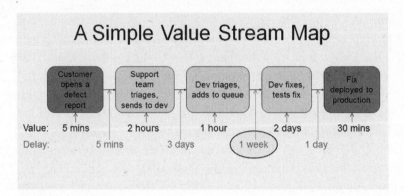

Figure 3-9: Value-stream mapping.

In our work with clients, we have also, where appropriate, leveraged some other frameworks and techniques, such as TOGAF[3] to address base enterprise architecture modification to support cloud adoption and Scaled Agile Framework (SAFe)[4], an industry framework to apply agile practices in an enterprise. Although these models can work, we have found that several established frameworks are not naturally suitable to the type of agile, rapid transformation that you are seeking. We have built a point of view that is grounded in lean principles and modern architectures such as microservices, as we discuss in Chapter 8 on Methodology. Clearly, cloud-centered frameworks are the way that we recommend you go when assessing your current state and defining your future one.

Step 4: Assess your organization's readiness

Up to this point, we have established a view of the key opportunities for cloud adoption, the highest-value business outcomes, and key gaps that require addressing to achieve the desired results. We have also shown you how to gather hard facts and data to support the measurable aspects of your cloud strategy.

To shape your strategy into something that can be executed, you need to shift your attention to organizational readiness. We recommend that you examine the following:

- **Cultural readiness:** Culture plays a critical role in the acceptance or rejection of any cloud strategy. Stakeholder buy-in, the ability to accept risk, new collaboration models, and new organization structures are all part of the transformation. How open will your organization be to the speed and scale of change required?

- **Resourcing readiness:** Can you realistically achieve your goals on time, using your existing resources? Understanding your current commitments is the key to making that determination. If there is time pressure, it is unlikely that internal teams will succeed in balancing business-as-usual commitments against the burden of cloud skills upgrade, planning, and execution. You must identify how you will mitigate this burden, what the skills gaps are, and what strategic and tactical roles remain unfulfilled. Outside partners, especially in the early stages of the transformation, can be tremendously valuable.

- **Budgetary readiness:** How is your organization preparing for cloud adoption? For cloud to succeed in the long term, you must be able to demonstrate improvement in cost control and financial forecasting. Your assessment of budgetary readiness is best done by using side-by-side comparisons of the true current portfolio costs and the projected cloud and cloud services costs. Leveraging Return on Investment (ROI) and Total Cost of Ownership (TCO) models will ensure buy-in and better expectation management. We have observed that it is both necessary and realistic to project higher operating costs in the early stages of the transformation. Ensuring that you follow an "invest to save" component as part of the strategy will greatly enhance your chances of success.

- **Technology readiness:** Beyond the critical aspects of the workload analysis we discussed earlier, the spectrum of technology readiness must expand to cover all dimensions of the portfolio. Technology readiness should include a methodical approach to assessing your condition in architecture, infrastructure, platform, and third-party-supplied services. Remember that your intention is not to try to remediate all the ills of the past; instead, the purpose of this analysis is to establish the readiness of your core building blocks to participate in your go-forward model.

- **Process readiness:** Many factors will challenge existing processes. To start with, enterprises are opting for speed, delivering services (versus products), seeking agility, dealing with new architectures (horizontal versus vertical), and leveraging new tools. Do you understand how to take what works for small startups and apply it at enterprise scale? Process readiness is not related just to the IT or line-of-business development teams, or just to the changes needed in the way they build, run, and manage their apps. Many other stakeholders are involved at scale: Security, compliance, risk, finance, legal, human resources, procurement, service desk, operations, and others all have a part to play. Is the organization ready for this level of process reengineering?

We explore these aspects in much more detail as we proceed through the remainder of the chapters in the *Playbook*.

Step 5: Build an execution framework with defined strategic milestones

The final step in building a cloud strategy is laying out an execution road map. The purpose of the road map is to establish the technology investment initiatives and to lay the groundwork for realizing your cloud vision. The road map serves as a baseline for reviewing the plan and the implementation strategy with the various stakeholders, thereby establishing a common viewpoint for communicating the business and technology strategy behind cloud adoption.

In this step, all the previous analysis, decisions, and conclusions are leveraged to outline a broad road map that supports the defined strategy. We recommend an execution plan that is anchored in the key adoption and transformation dimensions we discussed earlier. From an enterprise perspective, this plan not only addresses key stakeholder requirements, but also allows for understanding parallel execution paths and dependencies among tracks.

It is equally important to realize that cloud strategy road maps should not be static. These road maps must be updated as priorities shift or execution changes. We recommend that the defined strategy and its associated execution road map be reviewed on a 90-day basis and pivots made to accurately reflect progress, which better positions the organization for any future shifts in direction.

Figure 3-10 illustrates a high-level view of an execution road map for an enterprise client.

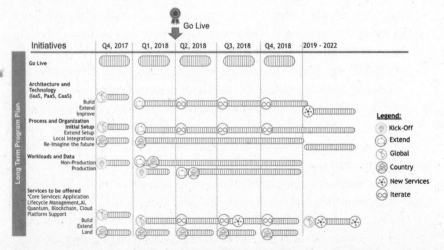

Figure 3-10: Client long-term cloud adoption and digital transformation road map.

Step 6: Define proven approaches best suited to your organization

Now that you have established your business objectives, understood challenges, assessed your readiness, and defined a broad road map, it's time to define how best to approach cloud adoption. We see two approaches at the end of a spectrum: a disruptive approach and an evolutionary approach. In some ways, a *disruptive innovation* approach can be viewed as radical, and the *evolutionary or sustained innovation* approach can be viewed as incremental. It is important to recognize that one is not better than the other and that either one can fit in an organization, which means recognizing the spectrum aspect.

When deciding how to implement cloud, you can use any of four policies:

- **Cloud First:** This is a policy that dictates that you look to the cloud before building in-house capability for the identified suite of apps.
- **Cloud Enabled:** This is a policy that dictates that you may use the cloud if you can get a better outcome than doing things the non-cloud way.
- **Cloud Connected:** This relates to situations in which you would never consider the use of cloud services. Systems with specific regulatory and compliance issues flat-out disqualify for cloud, for example, but you still need them to participate in a cloud ecosystem.
- **Cloud Only:** This relates to situations in which you use only cloud and never build it in-house. These are often non-critical workloads where you are taking advantage of the best of breed industry solutions or specialized services hosted in the cloud.

Note that these policies are not mutually exclusive. Over time, you may (and probably will) end up needing two or more of these policies.

In a disruptive approach, an enterprise typically looks to gain significant business benefits by aggressively leveraging public and private clouds, often as part of a Cloud Only policy. In this case, the transformation is modeled and spearheaded by targeting specific application suites, coupled with radical process and organization shifts. Timelines are relatively aggressive and the cost of failure is low, as the scope is based on acceptable risk and bound investments.

In an evolutionary approach, the typical situation is that IT deploys a cloud strategy that empowers business units and developers to embrace cloud. This approach is much more grass-roots. You may start with a Cloud Connected or Cloud Enabled policy in such a case. That policy must be grounded in maintaining some level of control and ensuring broader buy-in throughout the enterprise.

Figure 3-11 illustrates some common characteristics of the disruptive and evolutionary approaches.

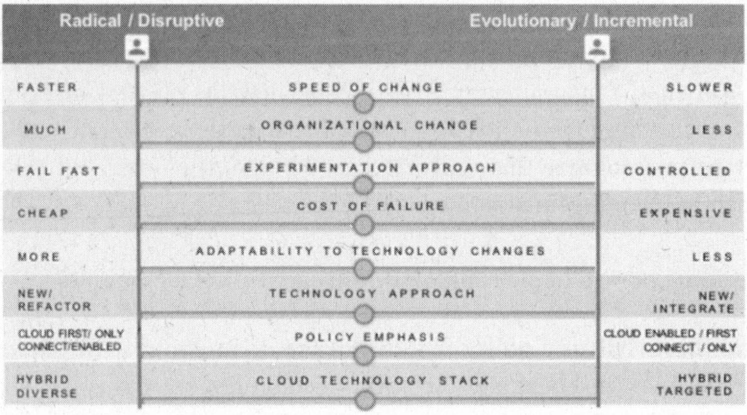

Radical / Disruptive		Evolutionary / Incremental
FASTER	SPEED OF CHANGE	SLOWER
MUCH	ORGANIZATIONAL CHANGE	LESS
FAIL FAST	EXPERIMENTATION APPROACH	CONTROLLED
CHEAP	COST OF FAILURE	EXPENSIVE
MORE	ADAPTABILITY TO TECHNOLOGY CHANGES	LESS
NEW/ REFACTOR	TECHNOLOGY APPROACH	NEW/ INTEGRATE
CLOUD FIRST/ ONLY CONNECT/ENABLED	POLICY EMPHASIS	CLOUD ENABLED / FIRST CONNECT / ONLY
HYBRID DIVERSE	CLOUD TECHNOLOGY STACK	HYBRID TARGETED

Figure 3-11: Proven approach in a spectrum of choices and decision-making.

Ultimately, where you fit in the spectrum of disruptive and sustained innovation is your organization's choice to make. The right approach is unique to each organization, as shown in Figure 3-12.

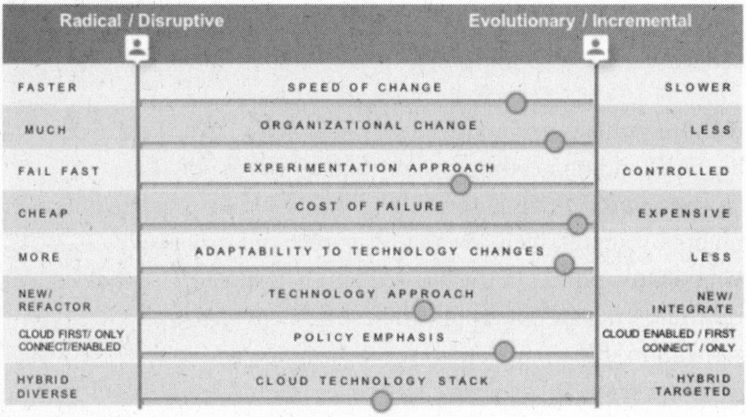

Radical / Disruptive		Evolutionary / Incremental
FASTER	SPEED OF CHANGE	SLOWER
MUCH	ORGANIZATIONAL CHANGE	LESS
FAIL FAST	EXPERIMENTATION APPROACH	CONTROLLED
CHEAP	COST OF FAILURE	EXPENSIVE
MORE	ADAPTABILITY TO TECHNOLOGY CHANGES	LESS
NEW/ REFACTOR	TECHNOLOGY APPROACH	NEW/ INTEGRATE
CLOUD FIRST/ ONLY CONNECT/ENABLED	POLICY EMPHASIS	CLOUD ENABLED / FIRST CONNECT / ONLY
HYBRID DIVERSE	CLOUD TECHNOLOGY STACK	HYBRID TARGETED

Figure 3-12: Each organization is unique.

Summary

Cloud adoption is a journey. As you embark on the journey, you need to establish a strategy for how your organization will adopt, transform, and deliver value. Then you need to turn your high-level cloud strategy into a tangible road map that you can execute. Using the adoption and transformation dimensions we discussed earlier, along with the key considerations and six-step plan, can help your organization benchmark its cloud maturity and identify the best approach for successfully adopting cloud.

The technologies used are only part of implementing a successful cloud strategy. An organization's structure and its willingness to adopt new technologies and to manage new operating models are equally important and should not be overlooked. Your organization can choose different approaches as adoption accelerates. You may start with a targeted disruptive approach and then ultimately move to an evolutionary approach over time, for example. Understanding your organization's options and guiding the business to deploy the cloud in a way that meets the business and technical requirements is the key to a successful strategy.

In Chapters 4 through 10, we take a deeper look at each of the key dimensions of cloud adoption and transformation, beginning with the role of culture in cloud adoption and transformation.

4

Culture and Organization

Every organization has its own culture, which evolves to meet the challenges presented by changing markets and industry growth. Business and technology transformations can falter on cultural elements, as organizations learn to adapt to meet these changing demands. This chapter shows how to identify the cultural roadblocks that can prevent your organization from successfully incubating a digital transformation.

What Does the Cloud Mean for Human Resources?

It may not seem that a technical decision such as adopting the cloud would mean much to the vice president of Human Resources, but the deeper issues that underlie why companies need to move to the Cloud are very relevant to your human resources leadership.

A recent survey by SilkRoad called "What Keeps HR up at Night," quoted in *HR Today*[1], states that the top issue for 53 percent of talent management professionals is creating an attractive organizational culture that will engage employees. That issue is closely linked to the third-most-important issue (41 percent of all surveyed), which is the ability to attract and recruit the best talent.

Other common issues that human resources executives face include dealing with interpersonal conflict, dealing with expressed or unexpressed negativity, and helping translate mission statements into actions that foster the organization's goals. All these issues have one thing in common: They are strongly influenced by the culture of the organization. If an organization can create a culture that values cooperation, that culture can lead to translating values such as empowerment, positive team spirit, and high standards directly into actionable results.

What Do We Really Mean by "Culture"?

An *organizational culture* is the combination of the shared values, beliefs, and social norms in an organization, resulting in behaviors, practices, and customs that the members of the organization follow. An organizational culture is formed and molded by internal and external forces acting on the organization; it reflects the history of the organization, sometimes derived from a shared mythology and the philosophy of the organization.

The values and beliefs that shape an organizational culture may be partially expressed through a corporate values statement or vision statement, but any organization often has as many unwritten rules as written procedures and policies. Organizational change is hard because change agents (either internal or external) usually don't understand these unwritten rules and hidden cultural norms well enough before they act to change an organizational culture. This leads to friction when the unwritten rules are broken.

An organizational culture provides the reason why a company embraces or rejects different practices. One thing to note is that organizational cultures are not homogenous; there can be different cultures at different levels of an organization or in different business units. Leadership at all levels also plays an important role, because a strong leader can have significant influence on forming a new culture or changing an existing culture. For that reason, understanding your current organizational culture should inform your decisions about implementing new development or operational practices and making technology choices.

One element that we must bring up before we dive into a deeper discussion is that this discussion is limited to the organizational changes that cloud adoption brings. This discussion fundamentally refers to the changes in an IT organization and, perhaps more important, to the changes in the way that the IT organization relates to the business. In any company, IT exists to serve the business. We assume that this relationship needs to be made closer and stronger. The relationship can be improved through incorporating rapid feedback and analytics so that the business understands the effect of decisions made within the IT context. Everything an IT team does should serve the business. If that statement is not true and obvious of your IT organization, then your business and IT team have more basic alignment problems that need to be resolved first.

What cultural elements make cloud adoption easier or harder?

We have found that several cultural elements make it challenging for a company to adapt to the cloud:

- First, you may remember from our description of the different dimensions involved in cloud adoption (see Chapter 2) that cloud adoption involves new elements, such as programming models; mechanisms for achieving resilience; and databases, frameworks, and DevOps tools. These new elements lead to new options for increased speed and frequency of deployment.
- Perhaps the biggest change is that cloud adoption fundamentally changes the way in which you deliver software. Among other changes, you must adapt to a new way of doing business with the companies that provide your cloud services — just one example of a larger mindset change that your organization must make.

As just one example of the reach of the cloud into the discussion of corporate culture, consider its effect on vendor management. Many companies have a corporate culture that, we can say, is very oriented toward short-term financial objectives. You may have a vendor management team that is involved in any purchasing decision, no matter how small. Now, we're not saying that vendor management isn't an important corporate function. What we *are* saying is that conflict arises when that team influences what should be technical decisions or rejects choices that do not meet corporate purchasing standards formulated for an older way of developing applications.

It is difficult for many vendor management teams to understand the nature of the cloud: The provider of a cloud service does not provide the same level of guarantees as a traditional hosting provider. Service-level agreements (SLAs) will be phrased differently and may cover different aspects because a cloud provider is essentially providing a service in the form of computing power, storage, and networking, not a full hosting and management solution. Thus, the contracts that many companies have with their existing hosting providers tend to be application-centric; that is, guarantees in terms of availability and other measures are written from the view of the application. Instead, the guarantees given by a cloud provider are in terms of services, which must be combined to support an application. This change in thinking often results in difficult contract negotiations, as vendor management teams must adapt to a new way of looking at what is provided.

This small example indicates a larger set of issues. You will encounter friction with teams that have existing ways of doing things that are ill adapted to the changes that the cloud brings. Adopting the cloud means that you can improve focus on rapid feedback between IT and the business and significantly improve speed of delivery. That opportunity allows you to press the reset button on what is sometimes a contentious relationship.

Many companies adopt the cloud to support innovation and rapid change, but those companies may not understand the fundamental cultural changes needed to make this adoption successful. In the following sections, we look at some of these issues and discuss how each cultural element affects overall cloud adoption. All of these different issues can be represented by an axis between two poles — in each of these cases we'll examine where your organization falls on that axis and what that means for changing your culture.

Willingness to embrace change

When you adopt the Cloud, you must realize that it will involve change: changes in your team members' skill sets, changes in your organizational structure, and changes in the way you fund and manage the cost models of your projects. More frequent and smaller releases mean that you will need to handle risk management differently.

A determining factor in how quickly you can make these necessary changes lies in how willing your organization is to embrace change. We have seen some companies that willingly embrace disruption; they view the ability to make rapid decisions and make quick, radical changes as an asset that allows them to respond nimbly to changing business conditions. Other companies are much more deliberate and slow about making changes; they want to examine decisions from many sides so that the cost effects and the effects on team members can be assessed completely.

We have seen that both styles can be successful, but each style has pitfalls. Teams that embrace disruption have to be able to determine how much disruption is enough. They fall into the trap of making too many changes at the same time and then rejecting them as a set when the results don't meet expectations. Or they don't give changes enough time to work before they reject the results of a set of changes.

Teams that are more deliberative, on the other hand, often fall into the trap of making plans that are far too detailed and complicated. This trap is often called *analysis paralysis* — falling into a loop of constantly adding one more level of review or another level of planning to any set of decisions rather than trying a controlled set of experiments to determine the outcome of the decisions. Teams also may miss the fundamental need to reassess their direction when business conditions change.

The cultural solution that we recommend avoiding both pitfalls is to make sure that you embrace change incrementally and make your decisions process data-driven — that is, follow the scientific method in your decision-making process.

When you want to make a change, such as adopting a DevOps practice such as test-driven development (TDD) or adopting a new container orchestration technology such as Kubernetes, first identify what measurable benefit you want to gain. In adopting TDD, for example, you may want to lower the overall testing costs or the total number of incidents reported by your users. In adopting Kubernetes, you may want to identify a metric such as the time it takes to deploy a new development environment for your middleware. In any case, you need to make sure that you track that metric or set of metrics for each decision.

By tracking metrics, you can determine whether a decision was the right one by determining whether your results match the expected outcome. This process works only when you can separate the results of one decision from another, however. In effect, you want to make sure that you are tracking independent variables and not trying to change too many variables at the same time. Now, we are not saying that all decisions to adopt cloud technologies or methods are completely independent; there is acceleration to be gained by adopting groups of tightly related practices and technologies. We talk more about that topic in Chapter 5 and Chapter 8.

Many changes, however, are relatively independent and can be assessed separately. The beauty of incremental decision-making is that by changing only a few elements at a time and then assessing the results of those changes, you can be more confident that you're not muddying the water by introducing dependent variables into your decision-making process. You probably could adopt TDD and Kubernetes at the same time, because they are fairly independent; the metrics around TDD adoption (Does your test coverage change? Does your development productivity change?) and Kubernetes adoption (How quickly can you stand up new environments?) are relatively disconnected from one another. If you were to adopt a new programming language such as Go or Swift into your team while the team embraced TDD, however, you would no longer be able to tell whether defect rates or incident reports are due to the learning curve of the new language and the team's unfamiliarity with it or due to the introduction of TDD.

In all cases, whether your team readily or hesitantly embraces change, one element that is absolutely required is leadership investment in that change. The leaders of your organization must act as change agents and put in place both the measurements needed to assess change and the safety net required to allow change to happen at the appropriate pace for the organization.

Decision-making style

Another key cultural element is how your team makes decisions. There are two poles of this axis, and although no company can be entirely on one pole or the other, it's still useful to speak of the extremes.

We call the first extreme centralized decision-making. In this kind of culture, decisions come from the top down. This culture is often characterized by a very hierarchical management style, with clearly defined and spelled-out roles and responsibilities for all positions. The advantage of this decision-making style is that decisions can be made very quickly. A key disadvantage is that as decisions work their way upward, they become further and further removed from the local knowledge that is needed to come to the right decisions.

The opposite extreme is consensus-driven decision-making. In this decision-making style, all team members are consulted or at least polled, and decisions are made jointly. The consensus-driven style tends to be common in more loosely structured organizations, especially those with very fluid team roles. The advantage of a consensus decision-making process is that all team members feel that they have buy-in on a decision. Everyone on the team feels that his or her input is valuable and that his or her voice has been incorporated into the final result.

Both approaches can work. Which style a team is more comfortable with may depend on the larger societal context in which the team is incorporated. In the larger cultural context of a team comprised of Californians in a Silicon Valley startup, versus a team that's part of a government-owned business in Southeast Asia, both organizational and societal cultural norms would have to be considered. Even these disparate extremes, though, have some common lessons.

The first lesson is that to be effective, a team needs a well-defined level of autonomy. That is, the team needs to clearly understand what level of decision-making and accountability it has. Not all decisions can flow upward; local knowledge is important, and even in a centralized decision-making culture, it's critical to define clear boundaries on the kinds of decisions that can be made at the team level and the ones that need to be cascaded up. Empowerment and accountability must go hand in hand, however. For a team to be autonomous, the members must also be able to deal with the consequences of their own decisions. Likewise, even in a consensus-based approach, team leaders need a way to break ties and make sure that the team doesn't become consumed by rehashing the same set of pros and cons.

A helpful artifact for either type of team is what is sometimes referred to as a work agreement. This artifact, which emerged from the Scrum community, defines the practices, rules, and disciplines that the team will follow. Even though teams can be successful with either type of decision-making process, it's important to make sure that the details of the process are communicated clearly. Even in a centralized decision-making culture it's important to make sure that in formulating the work agreement that team member input is taken in how its worded and phrased. Input into what disciplines and processes the team will follow is exactly the kind of local knowledge that ensures that the team will function smoothly.

Attitude toward risk

Another key cultural element to consider is the organization's attitude toward risk. Some organizations suffer from excessive fear of the unknown, which can be understandable, especially for organizations in mature or highly regulated industries. A culture of caution becomes a hallmark of the organization whenever any deviation from tried-and-true processes can be subject to scrutiny by regulators, auditors, or even peers. The problem occurs when this caution extends all the way down to the smallest decisions — when teams become afraid to try new programming tools, frameworks, or development practices simply because they are new.

Other organizations have a culture of always going for broke. We call the corresponding problem fear of missing out. In emerging industries or in highly competitive industries such as brokerages, where big bets are made every day, the problem is often not an excess of caution but an excess of recklessness. When every decision on every project becomes an opportunity to try the newest, coolest thing that someone read about online or heard about in a conference, it becomes difficult for teams to maintain enough consistency across or within projects to begin building reusable assets or to develop common operational approaches.

What lies between the two poles is the sweet spot for an organization. You want to allow local autonomy on small decisions while encouraging enough consistency across teams so that teams can work together. As we cover in Chapter 5, one of the roles of architecture in cloud adoption is helping teams set reasonable boundaries inside which they have technical freedom.

One of the most useful approaches that a team can take toward balancing the two poles of risk is controlled experimentation. It's probably useful to start by defining what we *don't* mean by *experimentation*. We don't mean randomly trying new things until something works; neither do we mean constantly changing tools, processes, or approaches in the hope that things will become better by some large order of magnitude. Instead, we mean that teams should carefully consider their process for working through a technical issue that goes beyond the expertise of the team and consider what to do about a problem that has two or more viable solutions. The term we like to use is limited blast radius. You want to limit the damage that a decision can make. Ensure that you define boundaries around each experiment in terms of time, money, and resources to limit the size of a loss in case an experiment does not work out. Also make sure that you define metrics for each experiment so that you can tell whether it is successful.

It is also important for teams to understand that not all risks are equal. Technical changes often do not have the same effect on the bottom line as business changes. An attitude of caution often applies on both the business and technical sides of an organization, however. Addressing undue caution through showing the value of incremental change is an opportunity for the IT organization to make itself more useful to the business and serve its core constituency better. By working with the business to learn how to implement small, incremental changes through the minimum viable product (MVP) approach that we describe in Chapter 8, IT can help the business manage risks while expanding into new or unproven areas.

View of failure

An area in which we see a cultural aspect closely related to the view of risk in an organization is the view of failure. On one side are organizations that view failure of any sort as a personal shortcoming. This attitude is possibly the most insidious cultural element that we see; it can poison projects before they start. On all the other axes we have seen, we try to help organizations realize that they either can be successful with the approach on either of the two poles, depending on how they make allowances for the corporate culture, or we try to help them find a balance between competing poles. This approach of either accommodation or finding a balance does not work with a culture that views failure as a personal shortcoming. A corporate culture that views failure of any sort as being the fault of the people involved and that punishes them for that failure (such as by bonus cuts, demotion, or firing) is one that makes it very difficult to adopt any new technology or way of doing things, cloud included.

Instead, in cases like this we need to move the culture toward a view that failure is something that a person and an organization as a whole should learn from. That view is the heart of many of the cultural elements we have already addressed. Only by trying new approaches and then learning how well they fit with a team's skills, personalities, and business constraints can any team grow and find ways of increasing its productivity and ability to execute. We have seen that people need a level of psychological safety to expand their capabilities. Only by providing a culture in which small failures are viewed as learning experiences can a team move on to larger, more ambitious experiments with potentially larger payoffs. Otherwise, fear of failure results in fear of the unknown, which can lead to overly deliberative processes and prevent teams from progressing.

Another approach that can mitigate this risk is to celebrate teams that take risks. If the team succeeds, that success is broadcast to the larger organization. If a team fails, that failure should still be celebrated as a way of learning and reinforcing the psychological safety net. Only in that way can teams learn to overcome their fear of failure.

CASE STUDY: SUBCULTURES IN A LARGE AIRLINE

It's important to note that corporate cultures are not completely homogenous. Even within a common corporate culture, you may have divergences or unique cultures within the larger context. It is possible for different teams within a company to embody different sets of values or exhibit different behaviors from the corporate culture as a whole. It's relatively common, for example, to have a development team that is very open to new ideas and that features a consensus decision-making style, as well as an operations team that leans toward more centralized decision-making and is more cautious about change.

When you're mapping out the path of the cloud journey that your company needs to make, you have to understand that different teams will move at different paces and that you may need to tailor your approaches for each team. In the following case study, we show how this approach worked with a large airline that we led on a Cloud transformation journey that took more than two years.

When we began working with the airline, we quickly realized that several distinct groups of stakeholders within the organization had to be brought on board with the changes that we were proposing for cloud adoption. These stakeholder groups included

- **Development:** Development had already embraced some parts of Agile development but was having trouble scaling those practices to the teams at large. As a result, the organization had pockets of Agile development; some people had more experience than others with and commitment to the principles needed to transform to an organization that would build cloud-native applications. What's more, those teams had a strong culture of going it alone, which resulted in many opinions about how Agile should be implemented. The teams needed a vision that would help them understand how skills and practices would be rolled out throughout the organization. The organization as a whole was very decentralized and already favored a distributed decision-making process, but individual managers of the teams sometimes clung to traditional top-down leadership.

- **Operations:** The operations team at the airline was not really included in the Agile adoption efforts. Its members were following traditional IT infrastructure library (ITIL) practices and thus were unsure what all the things they were hearing about cloud-native development meant for them. What's more, they had heard that the tools needed for managing a cloud-native implementation were different from their current tool suite, which also contributed to their feeling of uncertainty about the future. This team was small and already had a decentralized, consensus-driven style of decision-making, but its members tended to take their time analyzing new technologies from all angles before adopting them.

■ **Architecture:** The architecture team within the airline was also split several ways. Some of the team members were very much coding architects who viewed it as their job to build working examples of template projects; others were more traditional paper architects who viewed it as their job to provide detailed descriptions of architectural decisions. What's more, the team had no common vision of what set of architectural principles it should embrace and no common understanding of what its job should consist of.

As we worked with the client teams to help ourselves understand the customer, one thing we realized early was that each team embodied a different subculture of the overall corporate culture. At the corporate level, all teams abided by some strong beliefs and principles, one of them being that employees were the airline's most important asset. This principle made it improbable that we could solve staffing or skills problems by eliminating jobs or hiring new people; we would instead have to retrain people for new roles when those roles were needed.

A second basic principle was that speed was everything. This principle was just sinking into the organization; the airline had once held a dominant position in the industry, but competitive pressures had made it look old and stodgy to the press and customers, as it had lost its innovative edge. The chief information officer (CIO) was trying to push this new direction down to the teams and was rewarding teams that succeeded in innovating quickly with leadership positions, but many people within IT were stuck in the older, more traditional, cautious ways of operating suited to an older era.

Because of the many different subcultures involved, we realized that we were going to have to meet the teams where they were and tailor our approaches to the different learning styles, decision-making styles, and attitudes toward change that the teams embraced.

(continued)

(continued)

As a result, our initial plan, which set the course of the next couple of years, was the following:

- We realized that the most important thing to do for the architecture team was to help it develop a shared vision. As a result, we worked with the team in an offsite location to create a short list of common architectural principles for cloud-native applications that the overall project would follow. Then we worked with the team (and the development team; see the next item) to perform a shared four-week Proof of Concept (POC) to prove those principles and demonstrate directly what "Everybody codes" meant to the team. Those early successes helped team members understand their role in the new organization better and led them to embracing the guild model (see Chapter 8). Embracing the guild model allowed architects to be embedded in the development teams while at the same time giving them an opportunity to take on a point of view that is above the team-specific concerns and that allows them to help in coordinating team decisions.

- For the development team, the critical issue was understanding an Agile process for developing cloud-native applications that could be scaled to the larger development team. Within the POC, we introduced processes for sharing the wealth such as pair programming and TDD; we also introduced the squad model (see Chapter 8). The development team was impressed enough by the quality and knowledge of the IBM experts on the team that it decided to continue to bring in IBM experts on Cloud development to mentor team members full-time. The decision to not go it alone, but to form a partnership with an organization that had already gone through the process, was critical to the team's ongoing success.

- For the operations team, the biggest problem was understanding how it would be included in the cloud transformation journey. We took a different approach with this team by carrying out a design thinking session (see Chapter 9) to help them understand how to transition from their current processes to new processes based on modern techniques such as site reliability engineering (SRE). it was just as important for the operations team to sit with an established SRE team and watch how it worked.

Talent and flexibility

There is no question that when adopting the Cloud, your organization (IT and in most cases business as well) will have to change, because many of the challenges that the organization was created to address either do not exist when you are using the Cloud or are reduced in scope and effect. What's more, as we discussed previously, the ability of the cloud to change the pace of development means that you have different drives for speed and perfection, because the cost of changing direction is significantly reduced. These general principles lead to two changes in your organization:

- **You're going to need more generalists and fewer specialists.** This change is probably the biggest overall change for your organization. When you adopt the cloud, you will find that some types of current IT specialists are no longer needed, especially when building cloud-native applications. Also, you will find that the need for certain skills is reduced. Instead, you will need people who have skills in many areas. A single developer will be responsible not only for developing code, but also for building automated tests that validate the code, managing configuration automation that builds and deploys the code, and defining and building the operational automation (such as synthetic transactions or log configurations) that supports the operational infrastructure around the code. This approach, called full-stack development, is one of the hallmarks of the cloud-native development style.

- **Your organization will become less compartmentalized and more integrated.** The complexity inherent in building large IT environments has encouraged the specialization that the preceding item describes. As a side effect, many IT organizations have become very compartmentalized, with each silo responsible for only one specific set of tasks. Nowhere is this effect more pronounced than in the split between the IT operations and software development organizations. To react quickly enough to a rapidly changing business environment, these two organizations need to collaborate much more closely. In fact, in an optimal environment for cloud development, the organizations merge into a new organization called DevOps.

In general, both principles are about redistribution of skills and responsibilities. To be able to gain the speed improvements that cloud promises, organizations need to reduce the number of handoffs among teams. The problem is that these two principles — individuals take on more responsibilities, and teams change as roles move around in an organization — often lead to conflict in an organization.

Any time you propose a change in an organization, you will encounter resistance to that change. This resistance is simply human nature. Whereas some people seek out novelty, most people are conservative by nature and must be convinced that changes are worthwhile. This resistance comes in specific forms when considering changes in job roles:

- If you adopt a technology that eliminates a job role (such as your on-premises hardware team) if you move to the public cloud, you will face resistance from those who feel that their jobs will be threatened.
- When you introduce a new organizational structure such as a flattened organization based on squads (see "Basic Squad Organization" later in this chapter), you will face resistance from the managers and others in the existing structure who feel that their positions in the hierarchy or their spheres of influence will be threatened.
- Finally, experts who possess certain skills that are less needed may feel that they are no longer valued.

Organizations can follow a few strategies to preempt these types of resistance:

- Proactively offer retraining opportunities and reinforce the statement that the organization will make every effort to provide employees the opportunity to gain new skills that will be valuable in the new organization. This effort has to be a real effort. You have to not only offer the training, but also give people time to take that training without having it negatively affect their performance ratings on their current jobs.
- Offer managers whose jobs may be eliminated or made redundant by a flatter structure new opportunities for leadership in other areas. For many people, the same personality aspects that led them toward management and a leadership role often also lead them to take more risks and take on opportunities in new growth areas.
- Use the experts whose jobs may need to be spread throughout the organization more broadly to train and mentor the rest of the team members, showing that their skills are highly sought after and that they are not only still needed, but also valued in the organization. You want to create a pull within your organization; that is, you want to showcase successful parts of the transformation to make the transformation attractive. Showing off successes will make people want to be part of the transformation as opposed to fighting it.

Basic Squad Organization

One key element that we have seen to be important in cloud adoption is the adoption of an Agile approach that is conducive to the kind of rapid, incremental decision-making that the cloud fosters. Many organizations that have successfully adopted the cloud (including IBM itself) have followed a key practice called the squad model. The squad model, originally formulated by Spotify, formalized several Agile best practices that were nascent in many organizations in the industry.

The fundamental unit of the squad model is the *squad*, a small (usually ten people or fewer), independent team made up of a set of development pairs. We strongly recommend the adoption of the practice of pair programming for reasons that we will describe later in Chapter 8 on Methodology.

In our version of the squad model, we often find it necessary to have two general types of squads: application development (or build) squads and specialized support squads. Each squad is made up of a squad lead, who acts as an anchor developer and Agile coach for the squad, and three or four development pairs of full-stack developers. Each squad must also either include or have associated with it a product owner; it may also have an associated application architect. We also encourage squads to have a pair of dedicated site reliability engineers. In most squads that have a front-end (graphic user interface [GUI]) component, a designer should be associated with the squad, either as a full-time member or as a connection from a support squad.

We show an example of a basic squad in Figure 4-1.

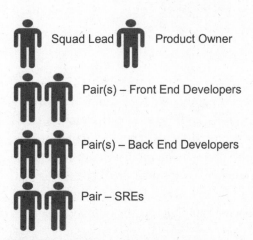

Figure 4-1: Basic squad organization.

Build squads implement *epics,* which are groups of related user stories. A single squad may implement one or more epics, but the smallest element of implementation responsibility for a squad is an epic. The user stories that define an epic are added to an ongoing ranked backlog of prioritized user stories. The organization may choose to use Kanban or other tracking methods to manage and maintain that backlog, but it is imperative that the backlog be kept up to date and reprioritized daily. This grouping of user stories into related epics is a natural fit for the microservices architecture that we will cover in Chapter 5.

A squad should be as self-sufficient as possible, which gets back to the principle we described earlier about needing more generalists and fewer specialists and to the more general principle that you want to avoid handoffs among squads. You can't entirely avoid the need for special types of skills in limited quantities, however. These associated roles may come from specialized support squads. One support squad might handle overall design and User Experience (UX) creation for your squads; this type of squad is often called the content squad. If a single squad does not have enough work for a designer, a good use of time is to allow a designer to support multiple squads. In Chapter 9, we will introduce another type of specialized support squad specific to systems management.

You can see examples of a couple of support squads in Figure 4-2.

Figure 4-2: Support squads.

We emphasize that squads are not only autonomous — completely owning an epic from end to end — but also co-located. Because pairs rotate (that is, people switch pairs from story to story), it is difficult, if not impossible, to separate pairs across locations. Although a project team can have multiple squads, each in a different location, the members of each squad should be co-located.

Pair programming leads to one of the key advantages of the squad model for our large-scale clients: It allows us to rapidly grow the number of squads that are both trained in the approach and familiar with the code and tests that are being written by fissioning the first sets of squads. It also allows new members to become productive very quickly as they undergo intense training in the code by pairing with more experienced developers. Thus, pairing spread expertise across an organization.

As a squad gains experience and maturity over a few months, you can choose to split the squad into two squads. One of the more senior squad members then becomes the leader of a new squad, bringing with him or her several squad members who can join with another set of newly trained developers. The original squad takes on new developers to gain experience with the squad's code and the IBM Cloud Garage Method (see Chapter 8) as the original squad continues to work on epics within the same application area. The new squad can move to an entirely new area or application as needed. In this way, the team grows over time while providing a path for developers within a squad to eventually become leaders of their own squads.

Finally, there is usually some need for project management and other coordination across squads. This management should be kept as minimal as possible; the goal of this model is to reduce handoffs and coordination. The project managers should act more as coordinators helping related squads find opportunities to work together than as project directors who micromanage the work of the people in the squad.

SRE model and squads

A critical reason why IBM and our clients have been successful in adopting the squad model is that we've simultaneously adopted another new organizational model: an approach that Google calls site reliability engineering (SRE). Simply put, SRE is a new approach to operations that is much more closely oriented to development than previous operations models. We cover SRE in depth in Chapter 9, but it's worth covering a few simple aspects of the model here, because it's such a key part of the way we propose that squads be staffed. There are two major sets of characteristics of a site reliability engineer:

- SRE is an engineering skill set. Site reliability engineers think of themselves primarily as developers, but they perform a specific type of development. That development is focused on improving the reliability, capacity, and manageability of the application.
- Site reliability engineers spend approximately 50 percent of their time addressing incidents that occur in production. This work follows similar

(but not identical) outlines as traditional incident management processes defined in the Information Technology Infrastructure Library (ITIL). They spend the other 50 percent of their time building automation (in terms of improved monitoring, event management, and so on) whose purpose is to keep production incidents from occurring again.

We believe that site reliability engineers should be incorporated into each squad as a special development discipline. We tend to recommend that at least two site reliability engineers be part of every squad, as we show in Figure 4-1 earlier in this chapter. Support squads of site reliability engineers can take on wider responsibilities than the individual epics (or microservices) that would support several build squads.

A reason why we believe that the SRE function is so important goes back to the ownership of user stories and epics by squads. Squads do not produce code and then completely throw that code over the wall to separate operations teams. Instead, the responsibility for keeping an application area (such as a microservice, described in Chapter 5, or an entire small application) up and functioning remains with the squad as a whole. SRE involves a special skill set that focuses on incident management and preventing, but the rest of the squad is also involved in handling problems as they occur. Thus, when bugs occur, the team will need to create user stories to fix the bugs and add them to the backlog along with the user stories for brand-new functionality.

Tribes and guilds

One final set of elements of the Spotify model that we recommend that organizations embrace is the notion of tribes and guilds. Tribes are an easy organizational construct to understand. If a squad is responsible for a single epic or a set of closely related epics, a *tribe* is a group of squads that are working on the epics that make up a product. It is often at the tribe level that you start to see the need for dedicated project managers to make sure that those squads work together smoothly and that everyone is working from the same assumptions.

One important thing to note about the pace of evolution to a tribe model is that the squad model is best applied incrementally. There's enough change in the move to a small-team driven method from traditional approaches that it takes time for people to become proficient with their roles in the new organization. We often start a project around a new product with a single build squad. Later on, we add new squads one at a time and create tribes only after three or more build squads are in place. Incremental growth is key. Trying to build a tribe of ten squads at the same time is almost certainly destined to fail, as lack of experience with the new job roles will lead people back to older ways of doing things.

A guild is a construct that's best understood pictorially (see Figure 4-3).

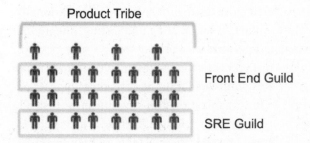

Figure 4-3: Tribe and guild organization.

A *guild* is a cross-cutting organization (and we use the word *organization* loosely; guilds tend to be informal and flexible) formed of people who share an interest or specialization. The guild exists for members to share information and experiences and to jointly establish common patterns and approaches.

Suppose that the product tribe as a whole decides to develop its user interface by using the React framework in JavaScript. The team may decide to establish an ad-hoc guild to facilitate the team members' experience-sharing as they come up to speed on the framework and decide on common patterns for the entire product. A more common type of guild that would last longer is an SRE guild. We often see SRE guilds formed and established for long periods to make sure that operational policies are established and followed across squads. Likewise, we recommend the formation of an architectural guild (see Chapter 10 for a more in-depth discussion of guilds) of all the application architects to decide on common development patterns for the squads.

Cultural elements of the squad model

The squad model brings some cultural challenges to organizations that are not familiar with operating within the kind of Agile mindset that it assumes. Each of the three major elements of the squad model can come into conflict with different cultural aspects.

Small

Squads are small teams of no more than ten members. A critical part of the squad model is that squad members carry out what would be thought of as several roles in a traditional software engineering organization. Developers in a squad, for example, perform much more testing than you would traditionally see in most development organizations. By automating unit testing, integration testing, user interface testing, and performance testing into a single DevOps pipeline, teams have much less need for the separate tester roles of traditional organizations. The testing role isn't eliminated, but the percentage of test and quality assurance (QA) people in the organization drops significantly. Instead, as the QA and testing roles become more distributed, the expertise needs to be spread to squads directly. In this model, the QA team (which becomes a specialized support squad) is much more concerned about planning and executing testing and mentoring squads than it is with the details of individual test executions. This difference in the way that QA and development organizations interact, and the fact that both organizations now come under the same squad leadership, is a fundamental change in organizations that have a strong culture of formal, almost adversarial testing performed by a separate group.

Autonomous

The level of freedom that squads have in determining their own priorities, outcomes, and iteration completion dates and even in selecting their own development languages and tools comes as a shock to many top-down, planning-oriented corporate cultures. Time and again, we have seen this situation become a barrier to cloud adoption that must be forced through by determined teams with the strong aid of upper management.

In one company that we worked with, we gained agreement to the use of squads as an organizing principle only to have the program management office tell us that the first thing the squads had to do was provide a description of the results of each iteration through the lifetime of the program, which stretched a year into the future! When asked why this was necessary, the stock answer was "So that we can do all the necessary planning to coordinate between the different squads for the entire program." These differing expectations — between the desire to see a detailed plan up front versus the desire to make decisions incrementally — began several rounds of explanations and negotiations about the definition and limits of the autonomy that the squads needed to be effective.

The key is that moving to a squad model shifts responsibility downward to the squads and away from centralized program and project planning offices. The program and planning offices need to learn to be more reactive and to work in an iterative way, which is difficult for teams that do not have experience with this kind of Agile development.

Co-located

Perhaps the single biggest change that we have seen in the past few years is a sea change in organizations' view of outsourcing and offshoring. In the United States and Europe, we're starting to see a backlash against outsourcing, as firms realize that software assets are an important category of intellectual property that a firm should be responsible for maintaining and creating on its own, just as it creates intellectual capital of other types as part of its core competency.

Software is everywhere now. The cloud pervades every part of people's lives, and any firm that thinks that writing software is outside what it should be doing will find itself quickly replaced in the market by more innovative firms that realize that the software is the critical factor. (Witness the demise of traditional taxicabs in the United States in the face of Uber and Lyft.) The result is strong pressure to insource IT development.

Going hand in hand with the pressure to insource is pressure to return to co-located teams to foster interteam communication. Even when organizations kept development in-house, they often moved it offshore to lower-cost countries. The problem is that the process of formal specifications, formal handoffs, and the inevitable miscommunication that resulted often ended up making development slower than it was been before the development was offshored. The result has been a second pressure toward having teams be on-shore and co-located in order to best foster inter- and intra-team communication and improve delivery speed.

Advantages of a COC

You may think that the squad model is a lot of change for an organization that's used to following a traditional model, and you would be right. That's why we suggest that you ease the transition by introducing a temporary organization into your company to provide the expertise and experience that you need to make the transition smoothly.

Introducing any new technology into a large enterprise is hard, and the set of technologies that makes up the cloud is no different. First, there's the challenge of dealing with the sheer number of people (often geographically distributed) who need to learn something new. Then there's the organizational inertia that any change must fight. Finally, there's the fear of disruption that change creates ("Will I lose my job if I'm not good at this?").

Enterprises need a way to smooth some of these technology and culture adoption bumps. Luckily, we can propose a time-tested approach to introducing new technologies that addresses these problems. That approach is a center of competency (COC). A COC is an independent body that is not owned by a particular development group, by the corporate architecture board, or by the operations team; it is supported and staffed by all organizations that have a stake in the success of a new technology. A COC is a managed entity with real priorities and deliverables, not a think tank to come up with new ideas, although a certain amount of research-and-development activity may need to be undertaken to make a new technology successful in an organization.

The COC develops common solutions and acquires new skills that are spread throughout the enterprise to increase the likelihood of successful technology adoption. The key point to be aware of is that a COC is not about supporting a single development project; it is about successful deployment of new technology at the enterprise level.

What are the goals of a COC?

The goals of the COC are to

- Promote best practices and standard processes that generate repeatable success
- Provide as-needed expertise to solve specific problems related to development and deployment
- Help teams become self-sufficient in knowledge and expertise
- Create a capability in the enterprise for looking ahead to new disruptive technologies and issues beyond the immediate focus of current projects

Life cycle of a COC

Although the COC is not a development organization, it is useful to think about the life cycle and activities associated with a software project as it moves from conception to production. The mission of the COC is to support all the stages of this life cycle, but from a specific perspective. Three phases of COC involvement are common:

- **Project conception:** At this stage, the business and development teams try to determine how best to address some business need. The COC can provide guidance on aspects such as tool selection and provide some insight into what is feasible within various time frames based on where the team is along the knowledge-acquisition curve versus how much it needs to accomplish.
- **Skills acquisition:** When a project begins, the COC members can act as mentors, trainers, and coaches to the project. The COC is helping team members gain new skills in the new technologies and solve the problems that they run into as the project progresses.
- **Knowledge dissemination:** When a new team is up and running, the number of touches required from the COC to the team probably will decrease, as team members become more competent with the new technologies and with the associated development and operations principles. Then the COC will work with the team members to provide opportunities to share what they've learned with others, capturing best practices and sharing experiences and successes through videos, blogs, meetups, and other avenues.

Likewise, a common responsibility of a COC is aiding method adoption. Adopting to the squad model and to a new methodology for Cloud development requires the expertise of those who have done it before. A COC is a perfect resource for providing teams that kind of hands-on expertise when they need it.

When a COC is not the right approach

COCs aren't perfect. In fact, they become absolutely counterproductive in several situations, including the following:

- **The COC becomes part of the problem rather than the solution.** COC members need a special type of attitude and personality. They need to reassure developers that new ways of working are possible and be sensitive to the disruption new technologies cause, at the same time pushing teams to new heights. They can't become advocates for why things can't change. If a COC team member starts identifying too much with a project's problems and isn't providing new ideas and solutions, that person needs to be disengaged in favor of a new COC team member.

- The COC becomes a political battleground or retirement home. A COC needs to be set up with specific goals and with a specific funding model, preferably supported by the chief technology or information officer. If a COC is not meeting those goals and can't consistently demonstrate value to the organization, it should be disbanded before it becomes another asset to be acquired in an executive-suite turf war.

- Just as bad as a COC that spends all its time in funding or political battles is one that is viewed as a sinecure for architects or project managers who are no longer involved in day-to-day development. A COC must be on top of the latest technologies and development principles, and the best way to achieve that goal is to have a mix of experienced and young members who can cross-pollinate and generate new ideas.

CASE STUDY: GLOBAL MULTINATIONAL BANK AND THE MEANING OF "GLOCAL"

The goal of our engagement with Global Multinational Bank was to act as a catalyst for accelerating their cloud adoption aligned with their business objectives. As we engaged with them, we learned that the organization was already well on their way on their cloud journey, but that journey had not always been smooth. Two big open questions for them were how to accelerate what was working well, and how to identify areas of friction that could use improvement.

This organization had a clear understanding of the global scale of their enterprise, which operates in over 10 countries worldwide, and the globally distributed end users of the IT systems. The key stakeholders we worked with included the bank branches in various countries, the lines of business responsible for financial products development, and the various globally distributed parts of the IT organization. The problem was that not all decisions could be made at the global headquarters; there were significant differences, not only culturally, but also in business priorities at the level of the country or region. Those differences were the reason why the bank had encountered issues in scaling small successes up to larger, global successes, and also why the headquarters team kept running into roadblocks with each new initiative.

Because of the global and local nature of the collaboration, the team coined the term *glocal* to emphasize the need for tight collaboration in all respects both globally and locally. This combination of global and local thinking had real organizational and cultural implications. It spurred the team to begin to reimagine all their existing functions.

The bank needed to create a vibrant, innovative, and can-do culture that tied the destiny of the global organization to that of the individuals running the business or participating in fueling innovation. The bank had to learn to think glocally to align their organizational strategic intent to the individual's participation in a culture of innovation. One way the team embodied glocal thinking was to establish a cloud Center of Competency (COC) as the custodian of programs to develop architectural decisions glocally and to scale the culture of innovation throughout the enterprise. A key lesson they learned in this process was that robust engagement and education programs were needed as part of this model. The enterprise established a Learning Academy as part of the COC to engage with, visit, and teach teams in each of the local countries to drive continuous reinvention as part of the culture of innovation. The result was that decisions could be made at the right level, and that the local teams better understood the reasoning behind global decisions — and how those global decisions could be adapted and modified to suit local conditions.

Summary

We have covered a lot of ground and a lot of concepts in this chapter, but this material is important in that it helps you understand the immense importance of culture change — and the difficulty of implementing culture change — as part of cloud adoption. All these ideas tie together into a logical, consistent whole. When we talk about the importance of metrics and a step-by-step, measured approach to change, we are laying the groundwork for helping you understand how organizational changes can be implemented. One thing you must change is the way in which teams and developers are measured. Within squads, you need to track measurements such as project velocity (how fast teams implement user stories) and systems reliability (in terms of the number of bug-report user stories submitted).

Also, putting a COC in place is the best recommendation we can give for building an organization that will be successful at embracing change, but a COC is not the right first step for everyone. Often, you may want to start (as our airline example does) with one or more small pilot projects to test aspects of how well teams will adapt to what is required in the cloud before you move to implementing a full COC.

In any case, we have shown you only the first step. Now you must understand how to put into place the technological and architectural framework that your teams will operate in, as well as the methodological framework that will support cloud-native or cloud-ready development in the squad model. These topics are the subjects of Chapters 5 on Architecture and Chapter 8 on Methodology.

5

Architecture and Technology

In Cloud adoption, successful software patterns are needed to build successful cloud applications. In Chapter 2, we introduced a framework for cloud adoption that introduced architecture and technology as a key dimension. Certainly, it would be the job of an enterprise architect to define these patterns, but the ultimate measure of a successful framework is use in projects. In this chapter, we discuss the role of architecture in modern cloud projects and architects are a crucial to set direction and guidance for cloud migration. We also describe how Enterprise Architects drive workload analysis when modernizing large numbers of applications.

What Does Cloud Adoption Mean for Enterprise Architects?

We often run into troubled projects that need rescuing. One of us recently took over a troubled cloud project — one of many cloud projects that were part of a digital transformation. Initially, the project was sized and executed for waterfall delivery. As the deadline approached, the client realized that the project was going to come in late and asked our team to take a look. To his dismay, not a single line of code had been written. There were many reasons behind this situation:

- The requirements were not finalized, so the project could not move forward.
- Decisions on development libraries and frameworks were not made; thus, the lead enterprise architect deemed that starting to code was a risk.
- The project executives did not trust new Cloud technology and therefore required early performance proof of architecture to validate the stack.

The client asked our team to take over, using the IBM Cloud Garage method in the hope that code would be delivered.

At the heart of this problem was that the enterprise architect was trying to deal with risk. The previous enterprise architects did not want to make incorrect decisions that could lead to project failure. As such, they approached every aspect of the project with extreme precision and caution. Over time, the list of deliverables they decided were absolutely required in order to proceed expanded into the following:

- Use case diagrams
- System context diagrams
- Component diagrams
- Class and object diagrams (even though Node was the programming language)
- Sequence diagrams
- Deployment diagrams

We want to emphasize that creating any particular architectural diagram is not a problem in and of itself. All these diagrams have their uses. However, when a team places more attention on creating the diagrams than the actual code to be delivered, it has lost sight of the task at hand.

Fast-forward to delivery, with a new team practicing the IBM Cloud Garage method (see Chapter 8 on Methodology for a detailed explanation). As we were staffing the project, the project manager asked, "Do we need additional architects?" The lead developer (who is also the application architect, though he would not admit to that) said, "We just need someone that can answer questions when issues come up".

The reason this was allowed is that this new architect had the credibility of being an architect who still writes code. After a couple of weeks, the team quickly realized that they could move very fast but had to take pauses to solve issues (as a reaction to things not working). Most of the issues were misunderstandings about technology details. The team started to wonder if they had gone too far in the opposite direction. The way that the new architect addressed this is to ask technical questions like, "Will this work in 2 different clouds" or "Are they testing performance enough in a Kubernetes environment". These questions were entered as user stories into the backlog (See Chapter 8) to force certain issues to be addressed.

This led to us asking ourselves "Is there a place for an enterprise architect?". The reality that hit us is that many times we become too focused on roles and responsibilities rather than solving issues. The right questions to ask are:

- Are there architectural issues that need solving on a project? *Yes.*
- Are there categories of architecture issues (application, Infrastructure, security, and so on)? *Yes.*
- Do we need specialized skills to handle issues? *Yes, but. . .*

There are many ways to solve issues. Some issues can be solved by a role expanding their knowledge (a developer learning a bit about operations and automation). Others may require deeper knowledge — subjects like security come to mind in this case. Certainly, having information about a particular area can come from well-documented patterns of success, but those patterns should not be buried in a 200-page document inside abstract pictures. Instead our key lesson learned is that architects should empower developers and site reliability engineers to make their own decisions based on patterns established in strategy and reference architectures. That job of empowering is what we will cover in this chapter.

Role of Enterprise Architects in Cloud Adoption

As enterprise architects empower developers and site reliability engineers to make more decisions during project execution, they can focus more on defining strategy for repeatable success. In Chapter 3, we talked about strategy from the perspective of the chief information officer (CIO) and defined dimensions including architecture and technology. Later in the chapter, we described prescriptive steps for developing a cloud strategy. An enterprise architect will be involved in all these steps but is needed to drive step 2, which is complete analysis of the workload portfolio.

During this phase, you need technology skills to determine how to handle the different workload types. Some large organizations may have hundreds of applications, so using tools to determine how to assess workloads is key.

Workload assessment

The first driver for assessing a workload is always the business requirement. Once it is determined it makes sense from a business perspective, we can assess the technical challenges. A good starting point to quickly assess a potential workload's general affinity to cloud computing is through answering high-level qualitative questions across a range of criteria.

This type of analysis can explore the following:

- How self-contained the workload is
- What the workload's scalability requirements are
- How standardized the underlying IT infrastructure is
- Whether the workload is available as an application or business process on the cloud
- How substantial the benefit of rapid application deployment for this workload is
- Whether the workload requires strong controls to meet compliance or regulatory requirements
- What the data transfer requirements for the workload are

Typically, the next step involves a more rigorous workload or portfolio analysis. Detailed information is collected on the existing infrastructure and software stack associated with the workloads of interest. This analysis requires detailed data collection on specific workload images, such as operating system versions and hardware specifications that include memory and storage resources, middleware, and software package information.

This detailed baseline information can be combined with nonfunctional requirements and existing operational costs to evaluate the potential fit for target cloud platforms. These types of assessments may also deploy auto-discovery tools for uncovering application connections and infrastructure elements. Some of those tools, such as Transformation Advisor, may analyze a particular workload based on a technology stack such as Java Enterprise Edition. (https://developer.ibm.com/product-insights/transformation-advisor). Some tools look at workloads from a more application-agnostic perspective and consider things such as performance and integration into other systems.

Typically, the more connections that are discovered or required, the less suitable the application is for cloud migration. In other words, the cost of migrating to cloud computing may outweigh the benefit. In this case, you might rewrite the application or decide to retire it.

Once you decide that a workload is a candidate for deployment on the cloud, the next challenge for the architect is determining your migration strategy. The driver for migration can also play a role. Figure 5-1 highlights mapping drivers to strategy and a typical percentage of workloads that might fit into that category. Your only reason for migration may be to help in automation for operations, to expose data for other new applications, or to enable quick releases and faster delivery of new applications and features into evolving spaces. The latter example means evolving into a new style of development such as cloud-native.

This approach has several key challenges:

Figure 5-1: Workload strategies.

- Complex cultural transformation limiting the scope and velocity of movement to cloud-native development and management
- Lack of integrated solutions and tools to build new cloud-native applications while integrating and evolving existing applications
- Operational challenges in integrating, managing, and securing cloud and on-premises applications and data

Figure 5-2 highlights the next level of detail in mapping the strategy toward a technology choice. As Figure 5-2 indicates, there are three main application migration strategies to consider, lift-and-shift, contain-and-extend, and refactoring. However, you also need to consider your data as well as part of any migration strategy.

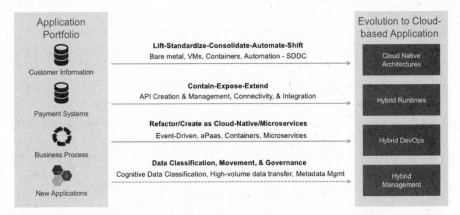

Figure 5-2: Application strategy.

- A lift-and-shift strategy might be simply moving your virtual machines from existing virtualization platforms onto a cloud but can also introduce new concepts like containers to achieve better automation and density with DevOps. However, we have found that lift-and-shift is rarely a simple movement of virtual machines. Most lift-and-shift movements also include some level of consolidation (such as eliminating unneeded environments or applications) as well as standardization (such as using the opportunity to build new virtual machine images on a common operating system and middleware base).

- In some cases, you might leave applications on-premises but expose them through an API gateway so that they can be consumed by newer applications. This is especially true of a strategy of containing costs by limiting additional feature development on applications that are costly or difficult to maintain. The API tier itself can be a new cloud application or an appliance.

- You may choose to rewrite or refactor existing applications into new cloud-native applications, which means adopting new cloud-native models such as containers or Platform as a Service (PaaS), or emerging technologies such as Function as a Service (FaaS). Figure 5-3 summarizes balancing speed of development, portability, and control in choosing workload standards.

- You cannot look at applications alone. Data itself may move, new database strategies may be put in place, and new database technologies (such as NoSQL) may be adopted.

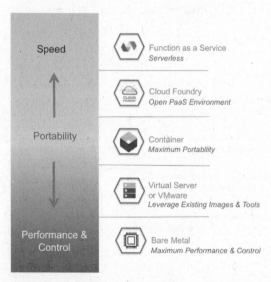

Figure 5-3: Deployment style.

Finally, it is worth noting the emerging space of private cloud. Just because you cannot move applications or data into the public cloud does not mean that you cannot adopt technologies such as containers. (See Chapter 7 for an example.) The private cloud market has shifted from its initial focus on Infrastructure as a Service (IaaS) to a focus on containerization. This shift increases the overall productivity of developers and enables DevOps. We see that clients are moving from on-premise virtual machines or hardware to containerized private clouds. Containerization enables infrastructure density in virtualized environments and consistent application development models from development (desktop) through production. Therefore, you have the added element of moving workloads into private or public cloud environments.

Figure 5-4 illustrates which types of workloads should run on a public cloud or private cloud, and which ones you should leave in place, but instead expose through APIs.

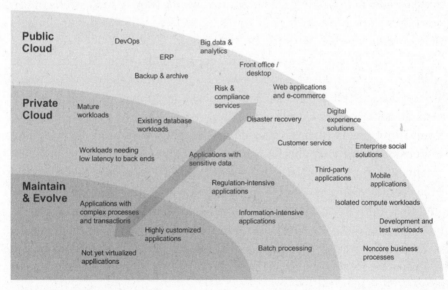

Figure 5-4: Cloud location.

After an architect has gone through this process, you may choose a few candidate projects to take on the journey.

Reference architectures

In this section, we discuss how an architect can build artifacts for a particular path, such as an architecture for a new cloud-native application using microservices approach to development.

All of us have worked on reference architecture initiatives that comprised several artifacts — lots of diagrams and text describing abstract concepts. Over time, through more diagrams and text, those abstract concepts were eventually realized. We've realized, however: Reference architectures have become self-serving; the artifacts exist only to be read by other enterprise architects. If the goal is to build something, is producing an artifact for other architects achieving that goal? An architect designing a building produces blueprints for structural engineers and contractors to use; he or she doesn't produce pictures to be consumed by other architects.

What should the real goal of an architect be? We think that it should be nothing more than building artifacts that allow the team to successfully implement user stories. We must draw some distinctions between the user stories that a product owner naturally creates and other user stories that are just as important. Product owners tend to focus on functional aspects, such as what a system does. An architect, however, should think about nonfunctional aspects: measurable aspects such as page-response time and aspects such as maintainability or manageability, which are harder to measure. Understanding, formulating, and capturing these requirements as user stories are important responsibilities of an application architect.

This viewpoint is one that we share with others in the Agile industry. In his book *Building Microservices*, Sam Newman writes, "Architects need to shift their thinking away from creating the perfect end product, and instead focus on helping create a framework in which the right systems can emerge and continue to grow as we learn more." Later in the same chapter, Newman compares the role of an architect with that of a town planner — someone who sets direction in broad strokes.

An application architect should be responsible for laying out the ground rules for how the squad builds its code, but the team should be able to grow and evolve the system as the implementation of user stories progresses. The architect acts as a boundary setter. He must survey. He must measure. Then he must build the fences.

Architect roles

As such, you must rethink the notion of architecture in software development. For architects to survive, they need to produce artifacts that target the builders of systems. The main job of an architect should be to develop artifacts for developers, administrators, site reliability engineers, and other team members. To do that, an architect must fit into one of two roles:

■ **Application:** *Application architects* think about the boundaries (specifically, functional boundaries and measurable nonfunctional boundaries such as performance) of the system being built. They build artifacts that a team needs to implement user stories within those boundaries. These artifacts can be language selection, framework selection, tool choices, code examples, and so on. An application architect should be a skilled developer and can even serve as the lead developer on smaller projects.

■ **Infrastructure/cloud:** *Infrastructure/cloud architects* thinks about the critical nonfunctional aspects of infrastructure, management, and administration and about what kind of artifacts the site reliability engineering (SRE) team needs to do its job. Cloud technology does not eliminate infrastructure challenges; the architect's skill set must evolve to include skills such as virtualization, integration, networking, security, containers, and storage. These architects also build artifacts for the SRE team to consume, such as event management tools and example code, and logging management tools and example code. We cover other types of artifacts in Chapter 10.

No one wants to listen to someone who has not been in his or her shoes. Therefore, an Enterprise Architect needs to have skills in development and operations beyond concepts. An *enterprise architect* is a decision-maker who has expertise in either development or infrastructure and who can view the big picture. That role is absorbed into one of the two roles above.

Components of reference architecture

The role of an architect in software, then, is to produce artifacts for developers, administrators, and site reliability engineers. How does an architect go about building reference architectures? A reference architecture should consist of repeatable patterns that solve problems that developers and administrators encounter. A modern reference architecture should be built as follows:

1. **Define a clear set of architectural styles.** Define and build examples within clear domains of areas (such as microservices and web development) that the team will work on.

2. **Define a clear set of nonfunctional architectural aspects.** These aspects are examples that ensure the completeness of a functional domain (such as security, resiliency, management, or availability).
3. **Convey your meaning by using only simple, minimal pictures.** Perhaps use only one picture with simple icons to communicate application flow.
4. **Provide example implementation artifacts in the language of implementers.** These artifacts can be GitHub pages of example code for developers, script artifacts for administrators, and so on.

Figure 5-5 shows an example set of architecture styles with the architecture domains. This artifact itself is not something that an architect would necessarily produce, but a checklist that a program manager would use to make sure that a specific area is completely covered. If you want to understand all the aspects of high availability in a microservices application, for example, you need to ensure complete coverage of that topic.

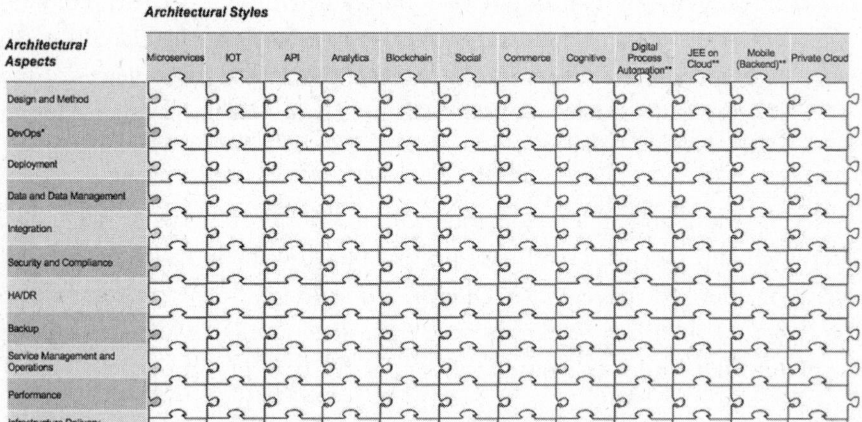

Figure 5-5: Architecture Styles and Aspects.

The best way to cover that topic is to produce an artifact such as "How to deploy a set of Java-based microservices using multiple databases across two cloud instances" (https://github.com/ibm-cloud-architecture/refarch-cloudnative-resiliency). This GitHub page displays a single architectural picture, as shown in Figure 5-6.

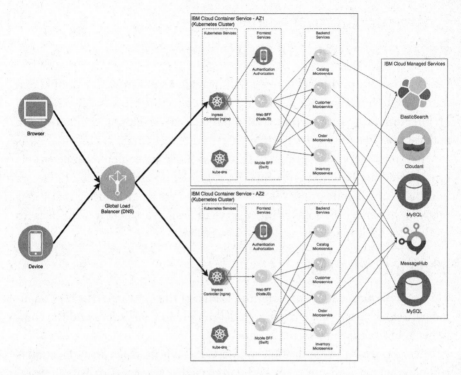

Figure 5-6: Resiliency of microservices.

Figure 5-6 communicates an important concept about resiliency, but it is useless if a developer does not know how to implement it. The GitHub tutorial has the following sections that explain what needs to be done:

- How do I configure a global load balancer across two cloud instances?
- How do I back up my databases with cloud storage?
- How do I set up data replication with MySQL?
- How do I set up data replication for Cloudant?
- How do I align security credentials across cloud sites?

The combination of a simple picture and implementation details give developers just the amount of information they need. The diagrams do not necessarily need to adhere to a standard such as Unified Modeling Language (UML); they only need to be understood by the developer.

Example Microservices Reference Architecture

For illustration, in this section we will provide an end-to-end example of a particular architecture style and some of its architecture aspects. Microservices architecture is an architecture style often used to develop new cloud-native applications. In addition, many organizations are rewriting existing monoliths into new microservices, because they want to move faster, deploy applications quickly, and not have to regression-test old code. If you look at the 12 factors of cloud-native applications (`https://12factor.net`), you notice that it has many of the same principles as microservices design; as such, it is the de facto method for building modern cloud applications.

Style introduction

This section does not go deep into the details of this particular style of documentation but discusses it in enough depth to help you understand the components of a modern reference architecture.

Microservices is an application architectural style in which an application is composed of many discrete, network-connected components called microservices. A Microservices architecture adheres to several principles, as follows:

- Large monolithic applications are broken into small services.
- A microservice is a small application that usually houses one function.
- The function is exposed through application programming interfaces (APIs) and/or messaging.
- A single network-accessible service is the smallest deployable unit for a microservices application.
- Each service runs in its own process at the operating system level. Sometimes stated as "one service per container," a microservice may run within a Docker container or any other lightweight deployment mechanism, such as a Cloud Foundry runtime that sets that process boundary.
- Each microservice should have its own DevOps pipeline.
- Each microservice can scale individually.
- Each microservice usually has its own database or owns a data model.

It is often useful to compare microservices with an older application style: monolith, shown in Figure 5-7. Monolithic applications grew out of a specific operational need. When servers were difficult and time-consuming to set up, it made sense for application server software to be optimized to run multiple copies of all applications. As each application becomes larger, however, the more brittle it becomes, so deploying new features to it becomes harder.

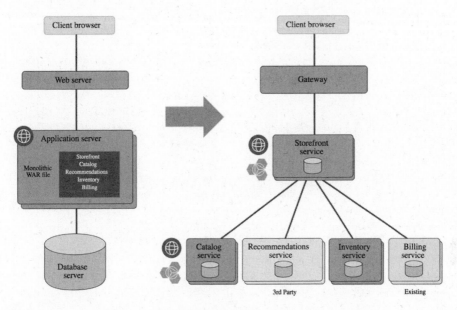

Figure 5-7: Monolithic architecture versus microservices architecture.

Martin Fowler's article on microservices (https://martinfowler.com/articles/microservices.html) is a go-to source on this pattern. You can also find a simple introduction to this topic at https://www.ibm.com/cloud/garage/content/architecture/microservices.

An example reference architecture

A reference architecture should be the entry point for a blueprint that allows developers and administrators to build a solution completely. Figure 5-8 shows a diagram that describes a complete picture of the areas you must think about in a microservices reference architecture. This is taken from IBM's Cloud Architecture Center (https://www.ibm.com/devops/method/content/architecture/microservices/0_1)

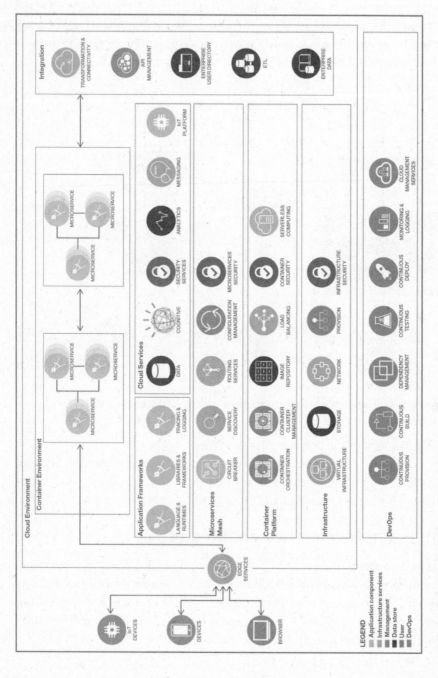

Figure 5-8: Microservices reference architecture.

In Figure 5-8 we describe various layers that are required to implement production-ready microservices. Having a top-level diagram such as we showed in Figure 5-8 is common to introduce all the different concepts that a reference architecture comprises. We will describe each of these layers in a little more detail in the sections that follow.

Container support

A microservices architecture should support the ability to run and orchestrate containers. Containers are the core technology for enabling microservices.

- **Container environment:** The container environment is where your microservices run. This environment is usually based on Docker images, but it can be based on other paradigms that use containers such as Cloud Foundry or a serverless environment such as Apache OpenWhisk.
- **Microservice:** An instance of application code running inside a container.
- **Replicas:** Multiple copies of a microservice used for scaling purposes.

Application frameworks

A Microservices architecture should provide the necessary support for application development. This includes all the pieces that a developer requires to build applications and run applications.

- **Languages and run times:** Microservice code can be written in many programming languages, such as Java, Node.JS, and Swift. Programming languages are supported by vendor-provided or open-source runtime environments such as buildpacks in Cloud Foundry. These runtime environments are built upon what is often called "middleware", such as application servers like Tomcat or Open Liberty, or other self-contained runtime environments such as Spring Boot.
- **Libraries and frameworks:** Microservice applications still require application frameworks and libraries created by an application architecture. Examples of these types of libraries and frameworks include:
    - REST frameworks such as JAX-RS
    - Dependency injection frameworks such as Spring
    - Unit test frameworks such as JUnit
    - Tracing and logging frameworks such as Zipkin

- **Cloud services:** Microservice applications can access a variety of cloud services. Examples include databases, caches, analytics, security, and messaging. Please review the IBM Cloud catalog (`https://console.bluemix.net/catalog/`) for examples.

Microservices mesh (service fabric)

A microservices architecture should provide a set of capabilities that enable microservices to communicate with each other. Examples of capabilities that should be supported in a service fabric include:

- **Service discovery:** The ability to allow microservices to be discovered and invoked. Examples include the Kubernetes domain-name service (DNS) service and Istio service discovery.
- **Routing services:** Intelligent routing services based on policies, access controls, rate limits, and quotas. Examples include the Istio framework.
- **Microservice security:** Security features for microservices such as secure service-to-service authentication with strong identity assertions between services in a cluster. Frameworks like Istio provide this layer.
- **Circuit breaker:** The ability to block calls to services that are not working and provide alternative actions. Examples include the Istio, Hystrix, and Failsafe frameworks.
- **Configuration service:** The ability to externalize configuration data from your applications. This feature is available in container orchestration engines like Kubernetes or is part of frameworks like Spring.

Container platform

A *container platform* is a system for automating deployment, scaling, and management of containerized applications. Examples are platforms built on the Kubernetes framework such as the Bluemix container service or IBM Cloud Private. A Container platform should provide the following services:

- **Container orchestration:** Automation for deployment of multiple containers.
- **Container cluster management:** Management of container environments as a service.
- **Container security:** Security features needed for container-based applications such as secret and key management, container scanning, and private containers.

- **Load balancer:** The ability to load-balance traffic to running containers.
- **Image repository:** Place to store Docker images used to run containers.
- **Serverless computing:** An environment that hides the underlying container and server layer and that allows developers to deploy code as event handlers to run in a managed fashion. One example is Apache OpenWhisk.

Infrastructure

A container platform does not stand alone. *Intrastructure* services provide the underlying cloud compute, networking, and storage capabilities that the container platform requires to function.

- **Virtual infrastructure:** Containers run on top of virtual machines or bare metal machines. In a managed container environment, this layer may be abstracted.
- **Storage:** Containers require the ability to store data, whether it be through object or block storage.
- **Network:** Containers must be able to communicate with each other. The underlying infrastructure must provide the ability to define isolated networks and network policies in order to implement container security.
- **Provision:** If you are running in a virtualized (virtual machine) environment, you need a way to provision new virtual machine images.

Integration

Microservice-based applications must communicate with systems that may run on-premises, in different clouds, or on different networks. Different types of Integration technology are required to invoke these systems.

- **Transformation and connectivity:** Secure connection to enterprise systems. API management is key, along with virtual private network (VPN) services. However, you don't only need to connect with or transform data in flight. Often you need to transform data at rest as well, which is the domain of database Extract-Transform-Load (ETL) tools.
- **Edge services:** These are security and infrastructure tools needed by consumers of microservices or other cloud services. An example of this would be a Content Delivery Network (CDN).

DevOps

DevOps is essential for successful microservice applications. Remember that DevOps is made up of Development-centric aspects and Operations-centric aspects. There are several different capabilities that a DevOps architecture must cover, beginning with several development-specific aspects:

- **Continuous provision:** Instrumenting and automating underlying virtualization, such as creating a Kubernetes cluster over a VMware environment.
- **Continuous build:** Continuously building Docker images required for development.
- **Dependency management:** Tools that automatically pull in dependencies during a build process. Examples include npm for Node, Maven, and Gradle for Java.
- **Continuous testing:** Automation for invocation of unit tests.
- **Continuous deployment:** Ability to deploy individual microservices into a container cluster.

We cover the following two operations-specific subjects in more detail in Chapter 9 on Service Management:

- **Monitoring and logging:** An underlying monitoring and logging ecosystem is required to allow for debugging systems and establishing the root causes of problems.
- **Cloud management services:** Cloud Management is a required discipline that encompasses many different tools such as Event Management tools and Notification tools. We cover this architecture and set of services in detail in Chapter 9.

Reference Implementations

As stated earlier in this chapter, the architect is responsible for creating blueprints for building a solution; therefore, a reference architecture without reference implementations is not useful for developer adoption. Providing the detail for building a reference application is key. Developers are among the most difficult audiences to please, but they are in an empowered position, especially in modern development. Developers must be convinced that a reference architecture is worth following; code is the way to convince them. Some of the reasons why developers are hard to convince are:

- Developers are religious about their technology and frameworks. They tend to want to use what they are familiar with unless they can be shown a better way of doing things.
- Developers feel that nothing is better than their own ways of coding. They must be convinced that new patterns and techniques are more efficient or productive.
- Developers need to be met where they are. Developers hang out in places like GitHub and Stack Overflow. Thus, providing examples and reference architectures in those places will contribute to the odds that developers will use them.

In IBM's Cloud Architecture Center, we store code and documents in GitHub. Most developers will like the ability to instantly download the code (by cloning a Git repository) and gain immediate access. Here is a link to the architecture:

`https://github.com/ibm-cloud-architecture/refarch-cloudnative-kubernetes`

We also provide a guided tutorial for beginners here:

`https://www.ibm.com/cloud/garage/tutorials/microservices-app-on-kubernetes`

How you publish information is very important to developer adoption. Using multiple styles may be necessary. A reference implementation should be detailed enough to solve the problems that developers need to solve but simple enough for them to consume. Figure 5-9 shows an example reference implementation for the architecture.

This reference implementation answers questions like "What application components are needed?" Figure 5-10 shows an example development stack used in a microservices application.

It is beyond the scope of this book to go into the details of all the technology choices that we use in our reference implementation. Instead we are providing it here as an example of a development stack; your own reference implementations should reach down to a comparable level of detail.

The reference implementations should provide guidance on deployment, as in Figure 5-11, which shows a page of instructions from the IBM microservices reference architecture Github repository showing how to deploy an application to several flavors of Kubernetes.

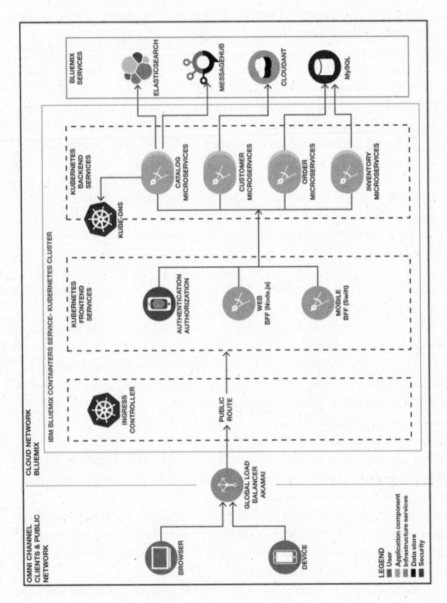

Figure 5-9: Reference implementation.

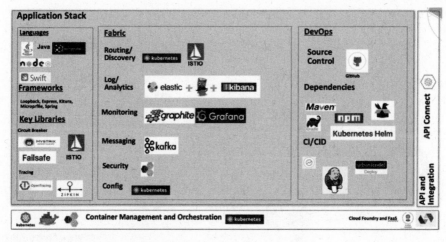

Figure 5-10: Development stack.

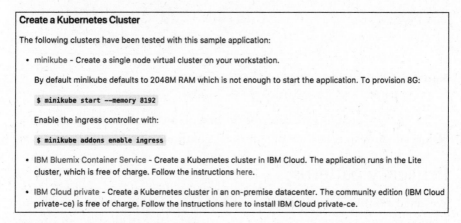

Figure 5-11: Deployment options.

DevOps implementation

DevOps, specifically automated continuous integration and continuous deployment (CI/CD), is important for cloud-native microservice style applications. Figure 5-12 shows an architecture for running a Jenkins configuration inside a Kubernetes environment for deploying Kubernetes-based applications (see https://github.com/ibm-cloud-architecture/refarch-cloudnative-devops-kubernetes#introduction).

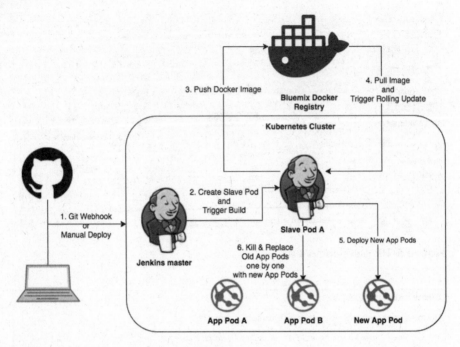

Figure 5-12: Continuous build and deployment.

The DevOps architecture describes what tools are used (such as Jenkins and Helm) and how to construct pipelines for continuous build and deployment.

Resiliency patterns

We used resiliency at the beginning of this chapter in the section on Components of a Reference Architecture as an example to illustrate the importance of creating artifacts for the right roles.

A reference architecture should provide guidance for getting the application into production and therefore should point to guidance on the details. Figure 5-6 earlier in this chapter shows an example of our reference application deployed for high availability and failover. It covers subjects such as the need for multiple instances of microservices, as well as the need for load balancers both within a container environment and at a global level across multiple clouds.

Security

A reference architecture and implementation should have the necessary details on implementing the security aspects of a solutions. For example, the GitHub page (`https://github.com/ibm-cloud-architecture/refarch-cloudnative/blob/master/static/security.md`) illustrates details around how you implement key features.

Chapter 6 discusses security and compliance in detail.

Management

Another key aspect of a reference architecture is how to operate and manage the solution after it is built. Many things done during build time are important for running the system. Chapter 10 is dedicated to this topic, so we will not go into much detail here, but it is worth noting that the reference implementation should provide details on how to stand up operations for a specific application.

For an example of how an operator or developer would create dashboards and integrate an application with a monitoring system, see `https://github.com/ibm-cloud-architecture/refarch-cloudnative-kubernetes-csmo`.

Summary

In this chapter, we discussed the role of architects in modern cloud projects. We discussed the role of the enterprise architect in both workload analysis and in cloud projects. We focused on how architects need to provide tangible guidance to developers and operators in the form of end-to-end examples with executable code in order to streamline development. Finally, we provided an end-to-end example of using a modern microservices approach to applications. In the next chapter, we discuss the importance of security and compliance in Cloud adoption.

6 Security and Compliance

Security and Compliance are two of the most misunderstood, and at the same time, crucial requirements of any application. Security and Compliance issues reach deep into every aspect of application development, deployment, and operations. Planning a move to the cloud should raise questions about how to best implement Security and Compliance in anyone's mind, but no one more so than the Chief Information Security Officer (CISO).

What Does the Cloud Mean to the CISO?

Chief information security officer may be the most thankless job in a large organization. Many development teams simply view them as the person who says no to new tools, new deployment options, and other improvements that they want to implement in their jobs. But if developers could spend a few minutes in their shoes, they would come away with a very different perspective.

It may seem to developers that the entire job of the CISO is to say no to them, but that's only a small part of the CISO's role. The CISO is responsible for ensuring that the corporation's technology assets — including machines, networks, programs, and data — are secure from unwanted intrusion, release, and misuse. That's a very wide-ranging job, which starts with formulating a vision of how to go about implementing information and technology security measures.

Cloud technologies are an increasingly important part of that vision and execution. Without oversimplifying the set of concerns that the CISO has about any new technology in general and Cloud in particular, any CISO will ask four basic questions about that technology:

- How does this affect my posture for compliance and auditability?
- How does this help or hinder me from protecting against data breaches and loss?

- Does this make it easier or harder for me to protect against distributed denial of service (DDoS) and other network-based attacks on my systems and application services?
- How do I manage identities and govern user access to my cloud applications?

Here are a few more questions that the CISO may not ask but should:

- What does a secure cloud-native development process and deployment look like?
- Will my people, processes, tools, and approaches change or remain the same?
- How do I get visibility to my cloud environment and applications?

We'll address the last question first and then go through the concerns one at a time before discussing secure cloud-native development and deployment.

Will My People, Processes, Tools, and Approaches Change?

The first question we have to discuss — whether processes, tools, and approaches change or remain the same, is sometimes not even asked. People often assume that things will stay the same. You must challenge this assumption when you're moving toward adopting the cloud. A security team works with a set of physical and intellectual tools, but those tools are based on a set of assumptions that you must examine.

Assumption #1: You can control access, security, and confidentiality all the way down to the physical hardware

This obvious but wide-reaching assumption leads to many security processes and tool selections that you have to challenge. In the Cloud, you do not control things down to the physical layer. Even in Infrastructure as a Service (IaaS), you don't control the physical hardware — only the virtual machines that work within someone else's physical infrastructure and hypervisors. As you move to higher-level constructs such as Platform as a Service (PaaS), Containers as a Service (CaaS), and Function as a Service (FaaS), you are abstracted further from the physical level, and the amount of control you can exercise in these models is reduced. You're at the mercy of the cloud provider, which affects the way in which you build solutions.

If a provider's FaaS offering is not certified for a particular industry standard that you require or is not available in all data centers for that cloud provider, you may be forced to change your application design or perhaps install and manage your own FaaS (such as Apache OpenWhisk) inside a provider's IaaS.

Assumption #2: Everything is contained within your network

Controlling access to a corporate network, both physically and through software, is one of the foundational principles of information security. In the cloud, this assumption is violated. In the end, this network is not yours. You are always working on someone else's network hardware and physical cabling. Routers, switches, and in some cases firewalls will be outside your control. What you instead must deal with is a set of bridges between your existing physical network, the cloud provider's network, and the public Internet.

Even a cloud provider's extension of your network, such as through a virtual private cloud (VPC) connected to your network through your existing Multiprotocol Label Switching (MPLS) connections) is not really your network, but an overlay on an existing network. The technologies such as Software Defined Networking (SDN) that allow this overlay to come with certain restrictions that you need to be aware of and that may result in changes in the way you manage or control network traffic.

A cloud vendor is not going to allow you to connect a hardware network sniffer to its physical network, for example. You must think of other ways to validate that traffic is flowing and being controlled according to your policies.

Assumption #3: Your team is responsible for everything

This assumption gets to some of the specific requirements of certification and audit that you need to require from your cloud vendors. The long and the short of it is that as you begin to use cloud services the roles in your team change. An analogy might be that as a provider of services, your role is like a plumber or electrician. Now, as a consumer of cloud services, you must begin to become more a general contractor, focusing more of your time and effort on ensuring compliance to specific regulations and industry standards. Some of the general standards you must insist on are things like SOC 1, 2, and 3 for ensuring proper controls on your data, ISO 31000 for ensuring a standardized risk-control process is in place, and ISO 27018 for ensuring proper controls on personally identifiable data.

Assumption #4: All your data must be stored locally

This assumption is obvious but surprisingly difficult to address. Although cloud vendors provide lots of data centers in lots of locations, you can't assume that for every solution, you'll have a data center available from a particular vendor in a particular locale. That situation can make compliance with data privacy and data residency regulations challenging. These regulations range from the very restrictive (such as Russia's requirement that all private data of Russian citizens be stored only on servers within Russia) to the much less restrictive (such as Nigeria's, which requires only that governmental data be stored within its borders).

If you operate in multiple countries, your solutions have to become hybrid, and perhaps multicloud, by default, which requires a close working relationship with your architecture team as you ensure that this kind of multicloud, hybrid solution is viable. Working within industry standards and not just de facto vendor standards is crucial.

Assumption #5: Your developers need to be security experts

In traditional enterprise architecture, security is often delegated to the operations or security team. Because the operations team already manages the infrastructure, it seems reasonable to ask the operations team to monitor the compute, network, storage, and application stack for any vulnerabilities. In essence, security becomes an afterthought rather than baked into the application design.

In the new world of cloud-native development, developers need to bake in security along with the application code, just like so many other nonfunctional requirements. In this new model (as we discuss in Chapter 5 on Architecture), a continuous integration and delivery pipeline is key to pushing out new code and features. Doing this securely and ensuring that your application is free of vulnerabilities means that developers need to take on some security responsibilities as well.

Your developers don't need to become full-time security experts to perform this task. Instead, they can leverage approved, hardened security services available from the cloud platform. If a developer wants to integrate authentication into his app, for example, he need not write custom code. A better solution is to leverage authentication services from the cloud with the appropriate configuration to add that authentication to the code.

Similarly, developers can take advantage of other security services available from the cloud to carry out tasks such as configuring network policies and scanning applications for vulnerabilities.

All these assumptions are just examples of a more general assumption: that everything is under your direct control. That's where thinking about the role of a security team is critical. Some things in the cloud are not within your scope of control at all. Service providers change their services frequently, for example. You can't assume that anything is static. Acting like a general contractor instead of like a service provider is the most important change in viewpoint. You need to work closely with your providers collaboratively — not in an adversarial relationship, but as partners.

How Is Cloud Adoption Affected by Compliance Issues?

Audit and compliance controls are increasingly critical for both cloud providers and cloud consumers. Auditors and risk officers need to validate implemented controls against an organization's security policy, industry standards, and risk policies, and report deviations when they occur. Compliance is defined by regulations (such as HIPPA and GDPR), certifications (such as FIPS), and frameworks (such as FISMA and PCI). Your organization may also add requirements on top of these regulations, certifications, and frameworks.

Certain standards are mandatory for specific industries, and an automated reporting tool can help organizations efficiently demonstrate compliance with these standards. Tools such as IBM Regulatory Compliance Analytics with Watson can help security teams understand their compliance posture. It's imperative, however, that cloud consumers understand how the cloud provider fits within their overall workload compliance assessment.

You need to manage your compliance needs in cooperation with your cloud provider. Different standards require different levels of interaction and often put the burden of proof for compliance on the cloud consumer rather than on the cloud provider.

As an example, consider the Payment Card Industry (PCI) Data Security Standard certification. The determination that a solution is PCI certified is an involved process involving an audit by an outside qualified security assessor. The problem with PCI certification is that it is performed on an end-customer solution, not necessarily on an individual component; all the parts of the system that can receive, carry, or transmit credit card data fall within scope.

As a result, many cloud vendors do not fully PCI-certify their products, instead guaranteeing that they are at best PCI-compliant (which is assessed via a self-assessment questionnaire). The burden of obtaining full certification of their overall solution is left to the cloud consumer. Most cloud vendors (including IBM) have security teams that will work with you to help you through the steps of PCI certification, but the process is lengthy and usually not cheap.

Although many other industry standards split responsibility for data protection, one new standard is an interesting exception. The General Data Protection Rule (GDPR) is a European Union mandate that is entering into force in 2018. It focuses on the rights of data subjects (those about whom data is stored) to be able to find out what is stored about them, request that it be changed or corrected where incorrect, and invoke the right to be forgotten. On the data-processor side, GDPR requires full transparency in data flow, accountability for breaches and violations, and harsh penalties for noncompliance.

GDPR (which may be the harbinger of data privacy rules in other countries in the future) requires significant new application functionality to allow data subjects to see what is stored about them and to request changes or the right to be forgotten. This situation reinforces the need for close collaboration not only with your cloud provider, but also with your architecture and development teams in an effort to meet these new requirements.

Next, you need to determine what actions to carry out to meet your compliance requirements. Implementing compliance management consists of the following set of activities:

- Defining and implementing compliance controls
- Monitoring and assessing conformity, and issuing an alert if a violation of a control occurs
- Assessment of and response (ideally, automatic) to violations
- Reporting and documentation of compliance information
- Validation by internal and/or external auditors via process walkthroughs and evidence evaluation

A detailed explanation of all the steps to implement compliance management is beyond the scope of this book, but you can find more information in the IBM Compliance Whitepapers[1].

How Do I Protect Against Data Breaches and Loss?

An organization's data is often its most important asset. If data is lost, compromised, or stolen, the effects on the business can be devastating. You need to have systems in place to protect data from unauthorized access, whether that data is at rest, in use, or in motion.

Data at rest is data that is physically stored on disks, tapes, solid-state drives, and other storage media. There are two vulnerabilities here: The data can be accessed, deleted, or modified by someone who doesn't have proper access rights, or the data may be copied to removable media. The way to address these vulnerabilities is through encryption of data at rest. Whether the data is stored in a database, a file, or other structure, it's important for the software or service that manages that data to store it in encrypted form.

Data in motion is data that is in transit between resting states, including data being transmitted over the Internet or between addresses on the corporate intranet. The Internet protocols offer a standard encryption solution — Transport Layer Security (TLS) — that is widely adopted and incorporated into higher-level protocols such as HTTPS.

Traditionally, data protection had to deal only with encrypting data at rest and data in motion. With the advent of the cloud, you also need data-in-use encryption to ensure that even if your compute infrastructure is compromised, your data is safe, and the cloud service provider does not have any access to your data. Technologies such as Intel's Software Guard Extensions (SGX) allow you to protect data in use through hardware-based server security. With SGX and similar technologies, application developers can protect select code and data from disclosure or modification. You can run your applications or containers requiring data-in-use protection on SGX-capable servers on IBM Cloud, for example,

A fundamental implementation detail of each of these types of solutions is that the encryption is performed with encryption keys. Therefore, it's just as important to securely create, store, and manage those keys as it is to use the keys to encrypt and decrypt your data.

Key management

As discussed in the preceding section, encryption performed with encryption keys makes protection of data at rest possible. A lost or stolen key can lead to data loss as surely as though the data was unencrypted in the first place. Likewise, you need to control access not only to these keys, but also to the unencrypted data. Thus, key management is a core component or service required to achieve this objective.

Using a key management service, you can enable the security benefits of Bring Your Own Key (BYOK) by importing your own root of trust encryption keys, called *customer root keys* (CRKs), into the service. Then you can use a CRK to wrap (encrypt) and unwrap (decrypt) the keys that are associated with your data resources, so you control the security of your encrypted data in the cloud.

The keys are protected by a cloud-based hardware security module (HSM). The HSM makes it possible for you to meet regulatory compliance requirements such as Federal Information Processing Standards. When keys are deleted, they can never be recovered, and any data that is encrypted under those keys can't be recovered. When you write applications, key management service providers program application programming interfaces (APIs) to generate, store, retrieve, and manage your keys independently of your application's logic.

Certificate management

Digital certificates are vital for data-in-motion protection whenever two parties who need to communicate securely need to authenticate identities, send confidential messages to each other, or generate digital signatures. Certificates are part of the common implementations of public-key cryptography. The public key of a public-private key pair must be made available to other users. This public key is made available in a digitally signed document called a *certificate*. A certificate, among other things, contains a user's name and public key, digitally signed by a *certification authority* (CA), which is an entity that issues digital certificates and is part of a certificate management system. When you connect to an HTTPS-secured site, your browser verifies that the website you are communicating with is legitimate by checking that website's Secure Sockets Layer (SSL)/TLS certificate, which is issued to a specific domain or subdomain by a CA.

At a high level, a certificate management system provides services that centrally store and manage your certificates. You upload a certificate that you obtained for your custom domain from a CA, the service stores it in an encrypted repository, and you get a central view of all your certificates and where they are in use. When you want to deploy or retrieve your certificate, you can use the service's API to automate the tasks. The API helps you keep track of when your certificates are going to expire so that you'll remember to renew them on time.

Finally, you need to make sure that the key management and certificate management services are integrated with your identity and access control services. IBM Key Protect and Certificate Manager, for example, are integrated with IBM Cloud IAM, so you can control access to keys or certificates with IAM policies. Likewise, with IBM Cloud Activity Tracker, you can audit certificate usage and management activities.

You need to add all these requirements together to form a complete data protection solution for your cloud environment covering data encryption, data access control, key management, and certificate management. You also need to consider the impact of data integrity on your overall system.

Data integrity

Data integrity refers to maintaining and assuring the accuracy and consistency of data over its entire life cycle. In our context, *data integrity* refers to protecting information from outside tampering. Hashing data, for example, allows you to detect when unauthorized modifications have been made in data. Database-related services usually have built-in data integrity capabilities.

There are two other major aspects of data integrity that come into play when you consider a cloud solution.

First is the important role of access control and audit. If you are building a cloud solution, you need to ensure that all data access and update is logged (something provided by your cloud database solution); you may also want to carefully consider the access control rights that are placed on your data and to whom they are granted. Even in traditional on-premises systems, this function is often a weak point, as many times, shared system IDs are given update and delete rights to the data modified by your applications. Thus, through your audit log, you may be able to determine the time and type of modification made to data, but you won't be able to connect it to who was responsible for the modification. If you want to be able to answer this question, a more rigorous access control policy that uses real customer IDs or embeds user identifications directly in your database records becomes important.

Another issue in ensuring data integrity is backup and recovery. All your data at rest should have a defined backup policy, as well as service-level agreements (SLAs) on recovery time and potential data loss. What's more, you need to ensure that the backups of the data are encrypted, that the keys are managed in the way we describe in "Key management" earlier in this chapter, and that the backups are stored in accordance with relevant data privacy laws. It may seem like we're asking you to dig deeply into the implementation details of your cloud services, but in fact, that is what is required to make sure that your data is secure and its integrity is maintained.

How Do I Protect Against Networking Vulnerabilities?

In the shared-responsibility cloud model, the cloud provider handles underlying network management, including network cabling and network device management (physical routers and switches).

The cloud provider's infrastructure provides basic, customer-level network isolation through individual virtual local-area networks (VLANs). From there, the cloud service provider typically gives the cloud consumer the ability to further isolate networks or systems from one another. You can further isolate your network traffic based on purpose (such as development/testing and production environments) and data sensitivity (such as regulated data versus public data).

Cloud-hosted firewalls

Purpose-built network security devices typically reside at the edge, or ingress/egress points, of a workload. These devices may include cloud-provider-ordered physical devices such as dedicated firewalls and virtual appliances such as gateway routers.

Cloud-hosted firewalls enforce settings that protect your environment at the Internet–cloud border as well as at the cloud-on-premises border (although the latter border is equally well protected by an on-premises hosted firewall).

Firewalls, including those at network level and web application level, are designed to prevent malicious activity from reaching your environment. You (or your managed services provider such as IBM's Managed Security Services) must define and implement the appropriate firewall policies based on the allowed or denied traffic for a given workload.

By blocking unwanted traffic from your environment, you can improve the performance of your entire system's network availability, workload, and security.

Intrusion prevention systems

Additional intrusion prevention system (IPS) appliances can inspect incoming traffic and analyze it for intrusion attempts or vulnerabilities in the workload components that would exploit an environment.

A combination of appliances and security intelligence monitoring helps protect your networks, workloads, and data from intrusion attempts and malicious threats. IPS appliances stop evolving threats before they affect your business. By monitoring security events and applying rules to block unwanted traffic and identified intrusion attempts, you can secure your workloads from network threats.

We recommend that you place an IPS device (along with a firewall) at the front of a workload so that your system can analyze allowed traffic for intrusion attempts and block any traffic that's identified as having malicious intent, as well as traffic from unknown or dangerous sources.

Incorporating security agents at operating-system level gives you additional security. The agents that reside at the OS level on a guest virtual machine or at hypervisor level offer a deeper defense. These agents have capabilities that are similar to those of network IPS appliances.

Distributed denial of service

Managed web defense helps you plan for, respond to, and correlate data during an attack, including a DDoS attack, which is designed to overwhelm you with the sheer volume of traffic.

Using cloud-based service providers such as Akamai or CloudFlare gives you a multilayered, robust approach to web protection so that you can minimize the effect of these types of attacks on your web presence.

A DDoS mitigation service can

- Offer inline DDoS protection on a massive scale for network and application layers with real-time threat visibility
- Detect and respond to parallel attacks with around-the-clock monitoring while blocking web attacks such as SQL injections and cross-site scripting
- Route traffic away from your infrastructure during an attack to help you better manage website availability and performance

Microsegmentation

As we discussed in Chapter 5 on Architecture, the practice of breaking services into smaller pieces continues to evolve. Where this practice intersects with security is the concept of microsegmentation. Microsegmentation allows you to granularly isolate cloud-native applications or data zones and securely interact with other services. With this level of distinction in place, you can apply fine-grained, workload-centric security policies and cluster isolation to protect containerized applications. As you build out complex microservices architectures on the cloud, microsegmentation at the container orchestration level allows those architectures to control access and routing to keep their microservices secure.

What Does a Secure Cloud-Native System Look Like?

When developing applications, you need to use secure engineering practices to build security into the foundation of your application. Following these practices prevents applications or services from introducing vulnerabilities, which are exploitable and present risks to customers.

These practices include

- Secure design that mitigates risks
- Secure coding guides and practices that prevent vulnerabilities
- Security testing to fix problems before the app is deployed and to validate that the product is free of known security issues

You must have all these components present in your development life cycle to ensure that the application you're developing is secure and free of vulnerabilities.

Consider a simple example that is compatible with the discussions presented earlier in this chapter and in Chapter 5 on Architecture. This example is a composite of several customer examples, but it shows the decisions that go into building a secure cloud-native application. Figure 6-1 shows an architectural diagram of this simple application.

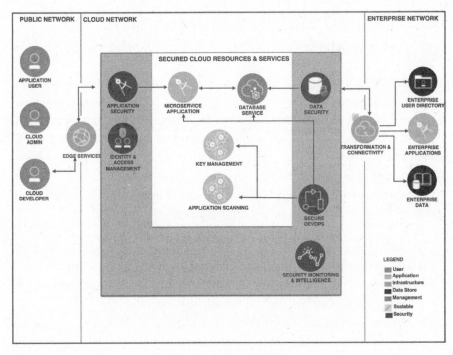

Figure 6-1: Secure cloud-native application architecture.

Starting from the front edge of the diagram, as we've already discussed, it's important to use edge services such as Akamai or CloudFlare to protect against DDoS attacks and other network-based vulnerabilities. When you are inside the Cloud provider's network, however, cloud firewalls and intrusion detection system (IDS)/IPS services provide an additional layer of protection.

Likewise, in the back half of the diagram, you see that data security is critical. Any data stored on the cloud needs to have the types of encryption applied in motion and at rest that we discussed earlier in this chapter and the data services needed to support identity management and data integrity.

Things begin to get interesting at the next level in from the Internet, with the services that are invoked before your application code (here represented as a simple microservices application). Identity and access management for your application is also critically important, as we discuss in the next section.

Identity and Access Management for Applications

The way that you choose to implement identity and access management in your cloud environment depends on your business requirements. You need to choose a cloud provider that supports the strategy you want to implement.

First in this section, we look at the key components of identity and access management. Then we explain those components and how you can implement them in your own environment.

To create a secure cloud environment, you need to account for the following components of identity and access management:

- **Authentication:** Enables applications deployed to the cloud to externalize the authentication of users to a range of identity providers
- **Multifactor authentication:** Combats identity theft by adding an additional level of authentication for application users
- **Directory service:** Hosts the user profiles and associated credentials used to access applications
- **Reporting:** Provides a user-centric view of access to resources or a resource-centric view of access by users

Authentication

Authentication, or an identity service, enables applications deployed to the cloud to authenticate users at an application level, based on a range of identity providers. Some of those identity providers may be:

- Cloud directory (hosted in the same cloud as the application)
- Social identity provider (such as Google, LinkedIn, Facebook, Twitter, or GitHub)
- Enterprise-hosted identity provider (such as a Security Assertion Markup Language (SAML) interface)
- Cloud-hosted identity provider

With the proliferation of SaaS and API delivery models, API keys have emerged as new sources of identities to accommodate.

Multifactor authentication

Multifactor authentication (MFA) — or additional authentication controls — is used to combat increasing levels of identity theft. Examples of MFA include single-use passwords, certificates, and tokens.

To maintain the user experience while improving login security, risk-based authentication controls are typically used. These controls change the level of required authentication based on a user's location, past activity, operation being performed, preferences, and other factors.

One common way to introduce multifactor authentication into your environments is indirectly, through SAML. The third-party identity provider implements MFA on your behalf.

Directory services

Directory services support the identity service by hosting the user profiles and associated credentials used to access applications. Directory services can be used to host a range of information, such as user identities and group or role membership, resource and service descriptions and locations, and access policies.

Directory services typically use a directory-access protocol, such as Lightweight Directory Access Protocol (LDAP), and can be shared across components in an application, across applications, or across organizations.

Directory services can be hosted on-premises or in the Cloud. Cloud directory services securely manage user profiles and their associated credentials and password policy inside a cloud environment. A directory service within a cloud means that applications hosted on the cloud do not need to use their own user repository.

Reporting

Reporting can provide a user-centric view of access to resources or a resource-centric view of access by users. The reports often address the following:

- Which users have access to each resource?
- Which resource is being accessed by each user and under what conditions?
- Which users make changes to access rights?

All three questions need to be answered by your security reporting solution in order to be able to fulfill basic auditing requirements.

Implementing identity and access for cloud-native applications

When you're implementing identity and access management for an application, the web application's audience determines the authentication model that you use. Table 6-1 details which authentication models work with which types of cloud-native applications.

Table 6-1: Authentication Models for Cloud-Native Applications

Application Type	Authentication Model
Unprotected website	No authentication is required.
Web or mobile application or APIs for an existing customer audience	Authentication is often handled by a SAML or Open ID Connect (OIDC)-based repository managed by the enterprise.
Web or mobile application or API's for a new customer audience	Authentication is typically handled by one of the social login options.
Web or mobile application or API's for business partners or suppliers	Authentication is typically handled by a SAML or OIDC repository.
Web or mobile application or API's for internal users	Authentication is typically handled by a SAML or OIDC repository.

In an ideal world, all cloud-native applications would secure all their endpoints, providing access only to authenticated users or services. Every request for an application's resources should know who is making the request and what access role and privilege the requester has.

The fact that sensitive microservices and resources are accessed from anywhere on the Internet heightens the need to establish the identity of a user with certainty, especially when users include other microservices, employees, contractors, partners, and customers. In a microservices-based cloud-native application, you want to ensure that identity management tooling and access control is in place to enforce business rules.

The App ID service in IBM Cloud, for example, enables applications deployed to the cloud to authenticate users at an application level, based on a range of identity providers. You can use the Cloud Directory capability of IBM Cloud App ID to add user signup and sign-in to your mobile and web applications. Cloud Directory provides a user registry for your applications that scales with your user base and includes simple ways to authenticate users to your applications by using email and password. It also provides the capability to store end user data, such as app preferences, or info from their public social profiles that can be leveraged in the app to support engagement.

Secure DevOps

As depicted in Figure 6-1 earlier in this chapter and getting back to the notion of building applications with secure engineering practices, we encounter a couple of subjects that can fall into the realm of secure DevOps. The first is a subject we've already discussed: key and certificate management.

It's incredibly common in microservices applications, for example, to use a technique called JSON Web Tokens (JWT). JWTs are an open, industry-standard method for representing claims securely between two parties as defined in IETF RFC 7519. They are commonly used, for example, to authenticate calls between JavaScript front ends running in a browser, and microservices back ends that process requests from the JavaScript. JWT works by using digitally signed tokens. Any time you have a digital signature, you have a key management problem, so secure key management becomes part of a secure DevOps process. Key management isn't the only practice of secure DevOps that application development teams need to follow, however.

As we state at the beginning of the chapter, the cloud is about continuous delivery, so automation is critical for your continuous integration and delivery pipeline to push out new code and features securely while ensuring that your application is free of vulnerabilities. As an example, a Kubernetes-based cloud-native application can be scanned for security gaps while running in production using Live Scan Capability with IBM Vulnerability Advisor. You leverage the built-in security scanning provided by Vulnerability Advisor that scans every image pushed to a namespace for vulnerabilities.

To ensure that your applications have followed these guidelines, use a service as part of your DevOps tool set that can scan your web, mobile, or desktop applications by using a variety of analysis techniques, including dynamic, static, and interactive analysis. IBM Cloud includes the IBM Application Security on Cloud Service, which detects application security vulnerabilities and recommends remediation actions.

Dynamic analysis

Dynamic analysis scans a running web application. If you enter a starting URL and user credentials (optional), the analysis will crawl the application to create a site map, run a battery of tests, and generate a security report.

The scan reports vulnerabilities, including details about the HTTP request and response information, so that you can understand exactly what data the test sent to your application and how your application responded.

You need to scan not only applications that are publicly accessible on the Internet (such as those in production), but also those that are inside your corporate firewall (in staging and other earlier development stages). You also need to scan applications that are not accessible from the Internet, which usually entails installing a tool that acts as a proxy in your network (such as IBM's Appscan Presence).

Static analysis

A static analysis reviews your application source code or byte code to review the data flow in your application. Static analysis can be used within a developer's integrated development environment (IDE) or automated as part of the build process. A static analysis detects where

- A malicious user may be able to introduce tainted data into your application
- How that tainted data flows through your application
- Where that tainted data may be used at a risk to your application

Static analysis shows you detailed, code-level information related to how the malicious data flows through your application. Your tool needs to be able to work with whatever programming languages your application team is developing with. For this reason, make sure that when you set architectural guidelines, you ensure that support for the languages you want to use is included in your corporate scanning tool set.

Continuous security and secure DevOps are not just about tools, but also about people and process. Security should be incorporated into the application's development from Day One, not added after an application is running in production. That said, you can still leverage the investments you have made in identity and access management, security monitoring, application and container security scanning, web application firewalls, and so on by embracing the secure DevOps approach and automating the integration of these tools into your DevOps process.

How Do I Get Visibility to My Cloud Applications?

Continuously monitoring each activity and event in the cloud is necessary for complete visibility of your cloud-based environments. You can gain the visibility you need by aggregating and analyzing logs in real time across various components and services in the cloud. Only when you have visibility across your IaaS, PaaS, and SaaS layers will you have a clear view of your cloud workloads and insights into any associated risks so that you can manage your audit and compliance processes. As a result, the CISO may want all logs and events to be integrated into the enterprise's security information and event management (SIEM) system.

As an example, IBM Cloud provides logging and monitoring as well as activity tracking services for providing visibility into your cloud environment. The IBM Cloud Log Analysis service allows you to centralize your collection and retention capabilities and to integrate with many industry-standard endpoints. IBM Activity Tracker allows you to monitor different types of cloud API access and use. These logs can be integrated into the enterprise SIEM. With such integrated insights, you can track how applications interact with cloud services, as well as monitor them for any abnormal activity and comply with regulatory audit requirements.

Summary

In this short survey of the types of decisions that must enter into building secure systems for the cloud, we've looked at how the role of a security professional such as the CISO, as well as the application developer, must change to be successful in the cloud. We also looked at questions that you must ask to make sure that you've addressed the main aspects involved in building secure cloud-native systems. Finally, we examined the question of compliance management and its effect on cloud adoption.

7 Emerging Innovation Spaces

Discussions of the role of innovation in the context of cloud adoption can go in many directions. You could talk, for example, about how cloud technology itself is an innovation, but for most of our customers, the need for innovation goes beyond the cloud. In many circumstances innovation is needed to determine how to use the cloud to fulfill a business need, especially in industries in which new technologies and ideas are disrupting the status quo. Discovering how new technologies and ideas can drive you to the cloud and solve business needs within a cloud and industry context is the next subject we will examine.

In this chapter, we discuss emerging innovation spaces. We begin the discussion by examining how innovation is a business driver and then give examples of several technology innovations, including data, analytics, cognitive, containers, and IOT.

Innovation as a Business Driver

In Chapter 1, we covered the role of several business drivers in hastening cloud adoption. We stated that technology in general, and cloud specifically, are only a means to an end. The end needs to be defined in terms of a business or mission strategic intent, such as achieving the following:

- Exceptional user experiences
- Accelerated time to market
- Higher service quality
- Cost flexibility
- Repeatability and flexibility
- Safety, security, and compliance with regulations

Innovation can often be a business driver in itself. The business drivers are about improving your ability to deliver within existing contexts. New ideas, however, can disrupt industries and create new contexts in which to operate. Location-based technologies in mobile devices, for example, became the catalyst for the car-service industry. Now you can request a car from a car-service company with your mobile device and find out exactly where that car is and when it will arrive. Other examples of how innovation works with business drivers include the following:

- **Industry:** Each industry has specific innovations that drive use of new applications. Examples include banks using image capture with mobile phones to deposit checks by taking pictures. Another example is the retail industry using location-based devices such as beacons to create a better in-store experience.
- **Efficiency:** Often, innovations that improve the way businesses or IT departments operate drive cloud adoption. For example, containers drive efficiencies in deployment and automation. DevOps is another example of a technology change that drives cloud adoption by improving efficiency in feature delivery.
- **Data:** A fundamental shift in how data is viewed has driven cloud adoption. In just a few years, the focus has shifted from how data is stored to how easily it can be accessed, analyzed, and presented. Now that data storage is cheap, the new goal is rapidly gaining insights from your most valuable asset: your data. For example, innovations such as new types of databases, new analytics approaches (such as deep learning), and new ways of displaying and navigating data drive cloud adoption.

Examples of Innovation

In Chapter 5, we introduced the notion of application styles as a way of categorizing the types of applications that you may want to move to the cloud. In this section, we look at some specific styles through the lens of innovation.

Data and analytics

Developers and data scientists need better ways to explore and deploy new analytics approaches that enable speed and agility. Within data and analytics application, development must change their approach by doing the following:

- Remove silos that are created by current organizations, systems, and tools to enable collaboration among teams and across technologies, from data scientists to developers.
- Take advantage of innovations emerging from the open-source and data-science communities.
- Break down artificial barriers imposed by a process or technology to enable self-service access to data across an enterprise while maintaining appropriate levels of trust and security.
- Enable insights made possible by combining multiple analytics technologies (such as the range of cognitive abilities in IBM Watson) to learn quickly from data and answer business questions faster than the competition.
- Develop the capability to rapidly build applications that deliver insights to production. The key to this capability is continuous improvement through rapid iteration, allowing teams to build smarter, more scalable applications in less time.

One way to view the changes in data and analytics applications is through the example of an e-retailer or online store.

When customers order online, they do so primarily for convenience and savings. These advantages make them willing to forgo the immediate satisfaction of inspecting an item in person, paying for it immediately, and leaving the store with it. When online shoppers receive merchandise that fails to meet their needs or expectations, their disappointment or the effort required for resolution can color their impression of the transaction, eliminating the perceived value of the convenience and the savings.

How can a retailer be proactive and retain customer loyalty? The answer is in data. In most cases, the data that is needed to address this problem is already present in one or more databases. This data includes product data that describes the products, marketing data that shows how products are promoted, transaction data that indicates who purchased which products, and return data that documents who returned a product and why.

A retailer can use advanced analytics on this data to identify both the products that are returned most frequently and ineffective marketing tactics that elevate the number of returns. By using statistical and machine-learning models, the company can take advantage of rapid alerts and automated information feeds on returned products to quickly identify problems with sales, anticipate problems before they occur, and resolve issues before they escalate.

A retailer can also develop customized applications that automatically contact customers who returned items and enable customer-service specialists to offer incentives to encourage those unhappy customers to purchase from the company again. This personalized, near-real-time response changes customer perception, which helps the company improve customer retention and loyalty.

In Chapter 5, we described architecture as one way of putting different technology areas in context. You can find an example of our data architecture on the IBM Cloud Garage Method site.[1]

The data and analytics architecture covers the entire data life cycle and ensures that data is secure at every step. The life cycle is defined as follows:

- **Preparing your data:** We show how to prepare your data by gathering, enhancing, and migrating it with leading-edge cognitive tools. The data can be structured (such as demographic and financial data) or unstructured (such as audio, video, and documentation).
- **Storing your data:** We give you guidance on how to choose the storage option that is best suited to your data. You can choose a traditional relational database management system (RDBMS) or one of several types of NoSQL databases.
- **Analyzing your data:** We demonstrate how to solve your toughest data challenges by using the best tools and the latest expertise. We understand that developers and data scientists do not want to invest in hardware and jump through software procurement hoops just to try new analytics tools. They are looking for a low up-front cost and a broad catalog of services that can fulfill most of their requirements. Cloud-based tools such as the IBM Data Science Experience, IBM Watson Analytics, and IBM SPSS provide a way to analyze data to gain insights, identify patterns and trends, and mine answers from volumes of data.
- **Creating your app:** We help you build smarter applications with embedded intelligence so that you can make decisions based on insights formulated by machine learning and cognitive functions. We show you that data-science and analytics applications are built with the same tools and techniques as other cloud applications.

Blockchain

Blockchain is an example of how innovation in the financial industry can drive business priorities. The blockchain concept emerged from the digital-currency movement, but the idea has matured into open-source projects and commercial products that can be applied to many industries. Any time a limited amount of trust exists among multiple parties, you can use the blockchain to create an environment that can eliminate fraud and create transparency.

Blockchain is a shared ledger technology that participants in a business network can use to record a history of business transactions that cannot be altered. The blockchain provides a single point of truth: a shared, tamper-evident ledger. This approach changes multiparty transaction tracking from a siloed model, in which multiple ledgers needed to be maintained and synchronized separately, to one that provides a single common view across the entire network.

Because blockchain uses consensus to commit transactions to the ledger, the results are final. Each member has a copy of the same ledger, so asset provenance and traceability are transparent and trusted.

Blockchain empowers enterprises in several ways:

- It allows them to leverage the power of ecosystems (such as partner and customer ecosystems) to complete transactions faster with greater trust.
- Applications rewritten to use the blockchain can reduce the cost and complexity of cross-enterprise business processes by eliminating inefficiencies, waste, and duplication.
- Blockchain can support the invention of new styles of digital interactions. It facilitates stringing together multiple interactions that were once isolated into a coherent value chain.
- It can help enterprises create cost-efficient business networks in which virtually anything of value can be tracked and traded without requiring a central point of control.
- Blockchain can decrease transaction cycle times by addressing risk and uncertainty while reducing fraud from e-crime and cyberattacks.

The blockchain reference architecture[2] is a good place to start to learn about blockchain.

The blockchain concepts are simple. A blockchain comprises three things:

- **Business networks**, which represent ecosystems of exchange, a supply chain, or a series of interconnected business transactions.
- **Assets**, which are anything capable of being owned or controlled to produce value. Assets can be digital or physical. A digital thumbprint (a permanent record) is created to connect the physical asset to the digital asset.

■ **Ledgers,** which are where transactions and contracts are digitally coordinated and encrypted. Ledgers are simultaneously and securely available to all participants with an audit trail.

To understand the value of a blockchain, consider a practical example. The diamond industry faces many challenges, including smuggling, fraud, counterfeit diamonds, and unethically mined stones. A blockchain can be used to mitigate some of those challenges.

The journey from mine to consumer covers a complex journey through legal, regulatory, financial, manufacturing, and commercial practices. Challenges exist every step of the way. Consumers run the risk of buying unethically mined diamonds. Governments must track diamond exports and pay export taxes. Customers want to be sure that they're getting the diamonds that they're paying for.

You can eliminate vulnerabilities through transparent transactions by using the blockchain. All parties have access to a secure, synchronized record of transactions. The ledger records every sequence of transactions, from beginning to end. In this example, a blockchain can record the mining, refining, and distribution of diamonds. The ledger keeps each diamond's records, including high-resolution photos at each block of the chain, from where the diamond is excavated in the mine to where it's cut and refined to where it's sold. The blockchain holds certificates of authenticity, payment transactions, and detailed characteristics of the diamond, including color, cut, clarity, carat, and serial number. A diamond's path can be traced from the mine to the consumer securely and transparently. At the end of a buying cycle, the diamond buyer has a complete, auditable, undisputable record of information.

For more information on how Everledger implemented this idea by using IBM blockchain technology, see Arvind Krishna's blog.[3]

Containers

In Chapter 5, we discussed microservices as an example of architecture and as a fundamental technology for cloud adoption. Within that architecture, we also discussed containers, which represent another type of innovation.

Increasingly, the cloud market is shifting from the initial focus on Infrastructure as a Service (IaaS) to a focus on containerization. This shift increases developer productivity and enables DevOps. Even for on-premises deployment, clients are moving from virtualized or traditional on-premises environments to containerized private clouds. Clients regard this trend as a safe first step toward embracing hybrid private–public cloud environments.

In this case, enhancing the productivity of development and operations outweighs the perceived total cost and disadvantages of a private cloud solution. Security must be built into the private cloud environment rather than added to it.

Containerization improves infrastructure density in virtualized environments and provides consistent application development models from development (desktop) through production. A driver of this market shift is the Kubernetes open-source container-management system. Kubernetes targets both operations staff and development. Containerization enables developers to treat configuration as code, enabling a modern DevOps tool chain. Using an open version of Kubernetes enables transparent deployment across the private and public cloud via the same containers.

Innovations in containerization, DevOps, automation, and operations have shifted modern IT to define new areas of focus:

- **Software-defined data centers:** Software-defined data centers use technologies such as software-defined networks (SDN), service catalogs, storage virtualization, and server virtualization and containerization to transform current data centers' infrastructure to IT as a Service (ITaaS) architecture.

- **Self-service provisioning:** Self-service provisioning enables the developer community to self-provision infrastructure, deploy applications, and tear down infrastructure after use. By leveraging a service catalog, you can enable end-to-end, on-demand, policy-driven, dynamic provisioning of IT services.

- **Cloud federation and capacity management:** You can build federation models to leverage service-provider clouds to manage burst-capacity workload needs. To do so, take advantage of automated monitoring and metrics for capacity utilization and forecasting.

- **Container management:** Technologies such as Kubernetes enable teams to build and deploy containerized applications with requisite management solutions, including scheduling, orchestration, and autoscaling.

- **Common management layer:** The underlying enabler of all these services is common management, handling tasks such as logging, monitoring, authentication, and role-based access. A common management layer creates a layer of abstraction that gives you better process portability across hybrid environments.

IoT

The Internet of Things (IoT) is the connection of devices to the Internet. Devices are outfitted with sensors, which gather data that reflects the human activities related to the devices and how the devices work. Sensors are embedded everywhere. According to Gartner.com,[4] 8.4 billion connected things were in use worldwide in 2017, up 31 percent from 2016, and will reach 20.4 billion by 2020.

Sensors can take many forms:

- **Measurement devices** such as thermometers and accelerometers measure real-world characteristics and generate numerical information.
- **Cameras and microphones** create streams of video and audio information that contain complex information about the world.
- **Beacons and load sensors** send out signals alerting of their presence, often detected by Smart Phones and other devices.

Data from sensors can provide valuable insights when the data is transmitted, stored, analyzed, and presented in useful ways. The Watson IoT platform provides a common standard set of protocols that devices can use to communicate with the platform over the Internet. After the data is received, analytics can be applied and made available to applications that meet industry-specific needs. Also, an IoT-enabled system can trigger an actuator as a result of an intelligent decision. Actuators can take various forms, such as relays that switch equipment on or off and displays that indicate when a device reports something abnormal.

Industries are finding many uses for IoT:

- Logistics and supply-chain management tracking of physical objects, such as packages and containers
- Smart buildings that are monitored and have control systems to manage their operations
- Connected vehicles that provide information to drivers on road conditions and vehicle status
- Medical applications that allow patients to be monitored remotely
- Retail applications that use information about a customer to tailor marketing and purchase recommendations
- Smart homes that allow consumers to control appliances remotely

IoT also creates opportunities for innovation no matter what business you're in. Better understanding your customers, their preferences, their movements, and their habits is a rich source of revenue opportunity.

You can use IoT for many purposes, including integrating structured and unstructured information from devices, people, the weather, and the world, and gaining insights from device information by using real-time streaming, predictive, edge, and cognitive analytics.

Furthermore, IoT can help you save money and avoid losses. Consider how IoT could be used within the produce section of a local grocery store. Think about what might happen if a refrigerator that contained prepared food failed. At best, the failure might cost the store money because of product loss. At worst, the failure might lead to the illness of a customer who purchased and ate spoiled food.

To use IoT to solve this problem, you might install temperature sensors in your store anywhere that food must be kept at a specific temperature. The sensors alone can't solve the problem, however. You still need to respond to sensor events.

Suppose that you receive all the sensor information, and as you receive it, you verify that each sensor indicates a temperature within a normal range. An IoT platform can analyze the incoming data in real time, test it against the expected results, and trigger an alarm action if the sensor is out of range. Because the alerts are automated, people at the store can act quickly to keep food from spoiling and fix any problem. The alerts can also be shown on a sensor dashboard where you can review and track all the sensor alarms from one place.

The IoT reference architecture[5] is a place where you can learn more about how IOT Solutions fits together, including industry examples.

Cognitive

Cognitive technology augments human expertise to unlock new intelligence from vast quantities of structured and unstructured data and to develop deep, predictive insights.

Cognitive applications interact with people in a natural way to answer questions and provide guidance that helps people make decisions. The applications understand a corpus of knowledge — a large collection of trusted information that could contain written material, spoken material, images, and video.

Two common uses of cognitive applications are

■ **Conversational applications:** *Conversational applications* are those in which a software agent (sometimes called a bot) converses in natural language with a human. (You can use the Watson Conversation service, for example, to develop applications that can converse with your customers.) You can quickly build, test, and deploy bots or virtual agents across mobile devices, messaging platforms, or even on robots to create natural conversations between your applications and users. Bots are hosted on the cloud and must be highly available. For more information about building cognitive conversation applications, explore the cognitive conversation reference architecture.[6]

■ **Discovery applications:** *Discovery applications* try to understand your data in several ways, extracting value from unstructured data by converting, normalizing, and enriching it. Then data scientists or other users can use a simplified query language to explore the data or to tap pre-enriched data sets such as the Discovery News collection. (Discovery News includes primarily English-language news sources that are updated continuously. More than 300,000 new articles and blogs are added daily from more than 100,000 sources.)

You can use many other types of cognitive services to enrich your applications. Services such as visual recognition, speech-to-text, text-to-speech, personality insights, tone analysis, and language translation can be added to conversation or discovery applications, or can enrich any other style of application.

Summary

In this chapter, we showed several examples of how innovation can drive cloud adoption. We discussed how new technologies such as containers, database technologies, cognitive services, and analytics can drive the move to cloud. The key that drives cloud adoption, however, is enabling a desired business outcome. Creating those business outcomes requires an approach to application development that fosters innovation at all levels. In the next chapter, we talk about the role of methodology in cloud adoption and how the IBM Cloud Garage Method can provide an innovation-fostering approach.

8 Methodology

A software methodology is something that sounds much more impressive than it is. A methodology is nothing more than a description of the guiding principles and set of steps that a team follows in developing a system. Every development team of every size follows some methodology, even if it is ad-hoc.

What we will introduce in this chapter is the lightweight software development methodology developed by the IBM Cloud Garage that we have successfully applied in dozens of client engagements, both large and small that we specifically built for guiding cloud-native development projects. We will discuss how our method came about, what practices the method contains, and provide examples and explanations of how those practices fit together into a cohesive whole.

What Does the Cloud Mean for the VP of the VP of Method & and Tools?

The idea of a comprehensive software methodology has a somewhat checkered past. In the late 1990s, object-oriented software development methodologies became all the rage, with multiple competing methods emerging, until the Unified Method and the corresponding Unified Modeling Language (UML) became accepted in the software engineering community. At that time, many companies set up large enterprise architecture teams and established vice president–level roles for methodology and tools.

Just as quickly as methodology reached its peak, however, it fell out of favor. Many companies were burned by the unfulfilled promises of big-picture methodologies, making them shy of the entire idea. What replaced the one big methodology was a plethora of methodologies calling themselves Agile. As a result, the job of selecting methodologies and tools has often devolved down to a director-level role, and in many cases, that task is just one job of the director of engineering or director of enterprise architecture.

To this person, at whatever level, the cloud is yet another complication. Navigating the complicated sea of multiple Agile methods, DevOps practices, and changes in technology is complicated enough. Especially in companies where shadow IT has led to decisions to adopt the cloud being made at the line-of-business level, the folks whose job it is to (supposedly) make decisions about software methods and tools often see the cloud as a threat to their jobs.

How does the person responsible for software methodology resolve these complications? That person needs a way to connect Agile concepts to DevOps concepts and put them in the context of a proven way that allows teams to take advantage of the features the cloud provides. This marriage of Agile and DevOps Concepts within a cloud context is what we provide in the IBM Cloud Garage Method. First in this chapter, we present a summary of the method; then we go into details on how the pieces of the method come together.

Introducing the IBM Cloud Garage Method

The IBM Cloud Garage Method is our approach that enables business, development, and operations to work together to continuously design, deliver, and validate new functions. The practices and corresponding tool chains cover the entire product life cycle, from inception through capturing and responding to customer feedback and market changes. We divide our practices into six areas, as shown in Figure 8-1.

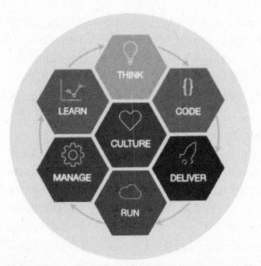

Figure 8-1: IBM Garage Method.

Culture

You may be surprised to find that the first of the pieces of the IBM Cloud Garage Method, the center of our approach, is culture. We consider cultural transformation to be so important that we covered the key aspects of it in Chapter 4. We believe that to be successful with the Cloud, you must transform your organization by combining business, technology, and process innovations to create teams that learn quickly from market experiences.

The key practices (covered in Chapter 4) that we espouse are

- **Building diverse teams.** To successfully innovate at scale, teams must know when to pivot and not become mired in groupthink. A healthy mix of diverse individuals is critical to building a high-performing team by providing multiple viewpoints.
- **Define organizational roles.** Developing cloud applications at scale calls for specific roles, each requiring unique skills and domain knowledge. We called out many of these roles in Chapter 4 and will call out an additional set in Chapter 10.
- **Work in autonomous co-located squads.** Teams perform best when they get to decide how to do their work, and they communicate the most efficiently when they are co-located. For these reasons, we follow the squad model of team organization, described in Chapter 4.
- **Adopt Agile principles.** Agile development teams produce software in short iterations on a continuous delivery schedule. Other Agile principles that are critical for long-term success are simplicity, a sustainable pace of development, and change based on customer feedback. We cover all these principles and how they are practiced in this chapter.

Think

As we built large-scale cloud systems and learned how to adopt Agile practices to enterprise realities, we realized that although Agile methods are critical, they are a necessary but insufficient condition for success. We realized that to incrementally deliver the right solutions, we also have to apply IBM Design Thinking and related design practices. The critical practices around this aspect of our method include:

- **Use IBM Design Thinking.** Design Thinking is a powerful, user-focused approach to innovation and brand differentiation that targets creating positive experiences. We discuss in this chapter why Design Thinking is so important.

- **Define a minimum viable product (MVP).** An MVP is the bare-minimum experience that your target persona accepts to accomplish a goal. The MVP is a critical part of the Design Thinking approach.
- **Hold playbacks.** Playbacks, which occur throughout the development cycle, gather feedback and keep the team in sync. They keep you from drifting too far away from the stated goals and desired outcomes of your project.
- **Plan iterations by using a rank-ordered backlog.** The design process results in a backlog of work, defined as user stories, which the squads must implement to deliver an MVP. The backlog is prioritized and used to plan iterations.

Code

To successfully build cloud-enabled or cloud-ready applications, your teams need to adopt development practices that help them release incremental function, gather feedback, and measure results. Some of these critical practices are:

- **Hold daily standup meetings.** Each day, the squad meets for no more than 20 minutes to discuss how things are going and whether any issues are blocking progress.
- **Use test-driven development (TDD).** Innovate faster by writing a failing test case and implementing just enough code to pass the test.
- **Practice pair programming.** *Pair programming* is the idea of letting developers work together, in pairs, at one set of keyboards and monitors to accelerate learning and deliver higher-quality code faster by doubling the amount of attention paid to each piece of code.
- **Continuously integrate.** By continuously integrating all working code, you can detect errors and integrate the entire system early. As a result, you can deliver code at any time.
- **Automate testing.** To deliver code continuously, you must automate your tests.

Deliver

It's not enough to just write code; your code must also be delivered into production. We show you in this chapter how to accelerate time to market by using continuous integration and continuous deployment, and by automating repeatable and transparent processes. We talked about these topics at some length in Chapter 5, but we address them in more depth both in this chapter and in Chapter 9. Two critical practices that we recommend are

- **Deliver continuously by using a pipeline.** To achieve continuous delivery in a consistent and reliable way, break the delivery process into stages. The goal is for the code to progress through each step with minimal human intervention.
- **Automate deployments.** Eliminate manual steps from the creation of the environments to the delivery of your code to production. Automation can be incorporated into the delivery pipeline.

Run

After you build and deliver working code, that code needs to run to be useful. We advocate several practices for running highly available, maintainable, and scalable solutions, whether they run on a public cloud, a dedicated cloud, or a private cloud, or in a hybrid environment. We discuss these issues in more detail in Chapter 9 on Management. The most crucial run practices are:

- **High Availability (HA) infrastructure:** Deploy to multiple data centers with the ability to fail over instantly if a problem occurs.
- **Dark launch and feature toggles:** Deploy new features to a subset of users for evaluation and feedback before going live to all customers. Features can be enabled or disabled based on parameters.
- **Autoscaling:** Implement autoscaling to ensure that enough resources are available at peak times and to save costs by reducing allocated resources during low-use times.

Manage

Next, you need to deliver operational excellence with continuous application monitoring, high availability, and fast recovery practices that expedite problem identification and resolution. Chapter 9 discusses all these practices, the most important ones being:

- **Automate monitoring.** Ensure that your application is available to your customers when they need it.

- **Enable fast recovery**. Develop a strategy to provide continuous availability and non-disruptive change.
- **Be resilient**. Test for the unexpected. Know how your application responds when someone pulls the plug.
- **Automate operations**. Automation enables you to reduce costs and focus your highly skilled staff members on high-value tasks.

Learn

Just as we believe that the place to start building cloud solutions is understanding the user through the IBM Design Thinking process, we believe that the process of learning about the customer never stops. You need to experiment continuously by testing hypotheses, using clear measurements to inform decisions, and driving findings into the backlog so that you can pivot when necessary. Two ways to learn about the customer that we advocate are:

- **Run A/B tests**. Compare two or more versions of a design or application feature to see which is the most effective. This method is a clear way to get empirical data so that you can determine the approach that works best and is most productive.
- **Drive development with hypotheses**. Developing hypotheses and testing them throughout the evolution of an application is key to delighting your customers. You must experiment continuously to find the right solution. Experiments must have clear metrics that validate the hypothesis or tell you to pivot to something new.

When we designed the practices of the IBM Cloud Garage Method, we drew on several industry themes. First and foremost of those themes was Agile development methods. We also drew on Lean methods (particularly Lean Startup and Lean Development) and from Design Thinking. To understand how these themes fit together in the Garage Method, you should understand why we believe that Cloud and Agile are a perfect fit.

Connections between Cloud and Agile

The cloud brings specific features to software development, including self-service resource provisioning; elasticity; the ability to pay as you go for computing resources; and the promise of rapid development, testing, and deployment through Platform as a Service (PaaS) technologies. Also, cloud services promise to accelerate or replace existing on-premises services with cheaper, easier-to-obtain services for specialized technology services such as performance testing and email.

You must have processes that allow you to take advantage of these new capabilities, however. You will not gain all the benefits you want if you must work within a tightly controlled, bureaucratic environment that forces you to plan everything up front and follow formal processes developed for a different set of assumptions about the cost and value of computing resources. That is where Agile methods and approaches come in.

Agile methods are a style of project management and software project organization that promotes iterative and incremental development. The basics of Agile methods were formulated in the Agile Manifesto, a set of four simple value statements in which the Agile community stated that it values[1]

- Individuals and interactions over processes and tools
- Working software over comprehensive documentation
- Customer collaboration over contract negotiation
- Responding to change over following a plan

The Agile community later clarified these value statements by developing a set of 12 principles that emphasized some specific practices such as early and continuous delivery of software, delivering software frequently, and valuing simplicity and technical excellence, as well as pausing occasionally to reflect on how to improve. Common features of Agile methods include concepts such as iteration through small, incremental releases; capturing requirements iteratively and in a lightweight way; and active involvement of business users.

These practices were driven by the people element in Agile methods, however, and you can bring about change only by improving collaboration between teams of business and technical people. You can motivate people only by giving them a working environment that trusts them to do the right thing. Likewise, adjustment and measurement are critical. You can't determine whether you're improving if you're not measuring how well you are doing, and you can't fall into the sunk-cost fallacy; the ability to change direction based on new information is critical.

For these reasons, cloud and Agile should go hand in hand. Agile methods enable you to organize your team in a way that allows them to take greatest advantage of the capabilities provided by the cloud. Likewise, an Agile team is most productive when it works in an environment supported by the cloud. The fewer roadblocks you put in front of your software development team, the more effective it will be.

Lean Startup and Lean Development

In 2003, Mary and Tom Poppendieck published the first of their books on Lean software development: *Lean Software Development: An Agile Toolkit*. It wasn't until 2011, however, that the Lean software development movement really caught on with the publication of Eric Reis's *The Lean Startup*. Many people were introduced to these ideas through Gene Kim's eminently readable 2013 book *The Phoenix Project*, which engagingly conveyed the ideas in the form of a novel about software development.

Lean software development brings the principles of Lean manufacturing (developed by Toyota and other Japanese automobile manufacturers) to software development. The first of these principles that these books convey is the idea that activities in software development produce real value or produce waste. *Waste* is defined as anything that is not of value to the customer. That definition implies a principle that is behind all the Lean methods and is incredibly important: Building a product the right way is all well and good, but you've done it all for nothing if you aren't building the right product.

Reis's book introduces a way to make sure that you always produce value for the customer: starting projects with an MVP, which is the smallest deliverable unit that can provide real, measurable value to the customer. What is clear in all the books on Lean development is the importance of following a process very much like the scientific method. You don't state requirements that are fixed for all time; instead, you formulate hypotheses and determine how to validate those hypotheses. You implement features that allow you to test your hypotheses, and you repeat the process iteratively.

The key is measurement. If you can't measure whether a feature is providing value to the customer, you are working from what may be an unfounded assumption about how the customer behaves. Measurement is just as important in the process of producing the software as it is in measuring the value of the outcome. If you can't measure how much effort, of all types, goes into producing a feature, you can't make reliable estimates about how much effort the next feature should take.

Consider your development process within the idea of a build-measure-learn loop. Learning is essential. If you're not continually learning about your customers, you may be working from unfounded assumptions about them.

The efficiency of building applications on the Cloud fits perfectly with this Lean approach. The less time you waste on repetitive activities such as acquiring compute resources, setting up middleware, and configuring networks or storage, the more effective you will be in reducing the amount of time spent on each build-measure-learn loop. Likewise, the cost structure of cloud — the fact that it is billed by the hour, day, or month — means that it's easy to change your mind about the structure of your compute infrastructure based on what you learn through each loop. No decision needs to be permanent, because you are not locked in through sunk hardware costs.

But to learn what your customers want or need, you have to know who they are and understand what they are thinking and feeling. In the IBM Cloud Garage Method, the missing piece that completes the Lean and Agile methods is Design Thinking.

Why Design Thinking Is the Missing Link

We believe that your software development process must begin with the simple assumption that the customer experience is critical. If an organization wants to be successful with its web presence, it needs to make the experience of every customer as pleasant and easy as possible. A world-class customer experience is important not only for customer satisfaction, but also for gaining and retaining customers and increasing revenue. What's more, the customer experience (or lack thereof) is often a strong indicator of how well the stakeholders are aligned, particularly the business unit and the team that implements the software. We believe that alignment is critical to building software that not only works as intended, but also meets the needs of the business in a meaningful way.

To fully embrace this principle, we strongly recommend adopting IBM Design Thinking[2] as a way of ensuring that all development is truly customer-centric and that everyone is aligned toward the same goals. Lean and Agile methods all promise to help you build and deliver quality software. But if you don't know who your customers are, you can't define what quality means to them.

IBM Design Thinking starts with the principle of the Loop (see Figure 8-2).

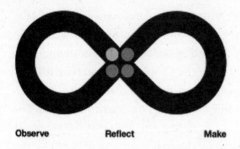

Observe   Reflect   Make

Figure 8-2: IBM Design Thinking Loop.

The Loop is a continuous cycle of observing, reflecting, and making. It embraces the idea of iteration from Agile methods, as well as the critical learning element of Lean startup. You'll see that ethos of iteration and learning throughout the practices that make up IBM Design Thinking.

Starting a Project with the IBM Cloud Garage Method

In the next several sections, we show you how the practices of the IBM Cloud Garage Method come together and how each practice flows into the next. Note that the example is an ideal case; every enterprise is different, and the IBM Cloud Garage Method needs to be tailored for each customer, as some practices apply better in some circumstances than others.

We begin with a set of practices that help you understand your customer. These practices come together in a Design Thinking workshop that brings together designers, sponsor users, business owners, and developers to reach a common understanding of how to meet a business need.

In the IBM Cloud Garage Method, we strongly recommend that every project begin with a Design Thinking workshop. This workshop ensures that everyone is in alignment on where they want the project to go — not only that they're building a product the right way, but also (and more important) that they're building the right product.

The first thing to do in a Design Thinking workshop is make sure that the participants from all the disciplines understand one another. We usually start with an exercise in which team members express their hopes and fears for the workshop so that everyone gains a clear understanding of what others expect from the process. That exercise fosters the important aspect of alignment.

The real work of understanding the customer begins with our use of the notion of personas,[3] expressed through empathy maps. An *empathy map* shows what a *persona* (a specific archetype of a customer) is thinking, feeling, doing, and saying. By understanding how various personas feel about and react to the system, designers and developers develop a better shared understanding of how customers will interpret design and implementation choices. But it's not enough simply to model an idealized customer; you must ground that model with real sponsor users to give you concrete feedback on your ideas.

Building the right thing requires obtaining ideas from the learning process. Discovering how to find good ideas is another major part of a Design Thinking workshop — we call this the process ideation.

Coming up with great ideas is one of the most important goals of a Design Thinking workshop. The key is knowing what ideas are important and likely to help the team further its agenda. The approach that we most frequently take starts with examining the current process considering the personas the team just explored. This exercise is called as-is scenario modeling. The team selects one of the most important personas from the preceding step. Usually, this persona is envisioned to be the most common user of the application, but this process can be repeated for different personas. From the perspective of that user, you identify a step-by-step scenario that outlines how she accomplishes what she will do today. The goal of this exercise is to find the current pain points, which help you understand what makes the experience most unpleasant for the user today and kick-starts your thinking about how to improve it.

Start by posting a large piece of paper on a wall. Divide the piece of paper into four horizontal rows; Label those rows "Steps", "Doing", "Thinking", and "Feeling". Next, outline your existing scenario by placing one sticky note for each step in the current scenario at the top of that large piece of paper in the "Steps" row, forming a series of columns. Then the other team members can begin using the information from the persona definition and empathy map to add new sticky notes in each column telling what the user is doing, thinking, and feeling at that particular step in the process. The result will look something like what you see in Figure 8-3.

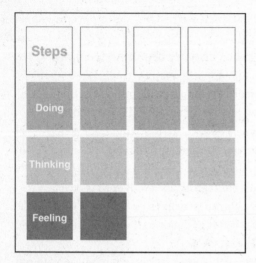

Figure 8-3: Modeling as-is scenarios.

This process is iterative. You go back and forth between things you learn about the personas in the as-is modeling scenario, and vice versa. Later scenarios may reveal things about earlier scenarios that you missed.

After the pain points have been identified, we start an idea-generation exercise to make the future user experience better. Each team member generates at least five to ten ideas to cure the user's pain, of which three should push against the bounds of realism, even to the point of absurdity.

Then we take all the ideas and classify them, using the axes "low to high impact" (Y axis) and "expensive to cheap" (X axis), as shown in Figure 8-4. It's important to have participation from the development team in this exercise; members of this team can help everyone understand the cost of implementation. This exercise is the moment to determine whether any of the concepts that fall into the "important but hard to do" area could be made easier and therefore move to the right. Concentrate your discussion on the far top-right corner. Ask yourself whether any strategic differentiating ideas could be made easier to implement. The ideas that fall into the two top-right areas are the ones the team should focus on as it works through the next steps.

The information gained through applying these aspects of Design Thinking results in a touchpoint that the team can rally around: the description of an MVP. As discussed earlier, an MVP is the smallest, most tightly focused description of what a team can deliver and still deliver measurable customer value. For each big idea, you need to identify the key hypotheses that the idea represents. An MVP is a critical concept. The Design Thinking workshop process is rapid (a matter of a few days), and an MVP definition is written to be developed and rolled out to customers rapidly — in weeks rather than months. This process helps developers introduce new features rapidly and obtain feedback quickly, which allows the team to prove or disprove its hypotheses. Based on increased insight, the team should formulate a set of related hypotheses and user experiments to be run that will help it understand how to validate the MVP.

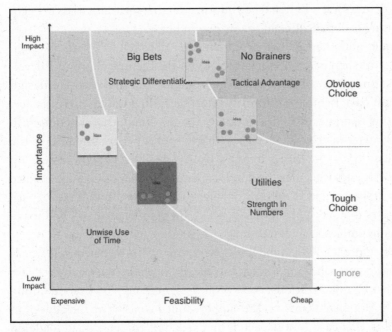

Figure 8-4: Prioritizing ideas.

At this point, alignment comes into play again. One exercise that we frequently use in the Design Thinking workshop helps the team decide what the goals and nongoals of the entire product will be. This exercise is important for helping the team understand the agendas that team members bring to the project. Developers may want to explore new cloud technologies such as PaaS, for example, but the product owner may be concerned only with delivering the first features on time. This exercise gives the team an opportunity to bring these desires out in a nonconfrontational way so that the team can sort through the pros and cons of each potential goal. Agreeing on goals and nongoals ensures that the team set the right priorities in the MVP definition and helps guide some later discussions.

Wrapping Up the Workshop

One place where the IBM Cloud Garage approach differs from other Agile methods and from the basic outlines of IBM Design Thinking is that at this point, you are ready to consider some key architectural issues. We have found that following up a Design Thinking session with a quick (half-day) architectural discussion allows the business and technical teams to come into closer alignment on the best approach for implementing the MVP. This discussion also helps define some additional key information that the team needs to begin implementing the application at the inception phase.

We should note that the role of the designer does not end with a Design Thinking workshop but continues throughout the lifetime of product development. At this point, different skills can begin to come into play. The design team should have the input it needs to start designing the user experience. Initially, this team needs to develop only the minimum that is required to validate the user-interface concepts with the sponsor users and to give the development team something to work from. Later, the designers develop detailed wireframes and guide the development of the detailed User Experience (UX). The designers and the product owner then review the wireframes with sponsor users in a set of playbacks in which they gather feedback and make changes in hypotheses and wireframes.

The best approach is to embed designers directly into your development squads. That approach is not always feasible, however, because designers are rare in most IT organizations, so several designers may be shared among multiple development teams via the support squad concept we introduced in Chapter 4. In that case, you have a design squad or content squad made up of the shared designers.

Our Approach to Project Inception

In Chapter 4, we described the role of the squad lead — the lead developer for the project. The squad lead and other developers must take part in the Design Thinking workshop so that they understand the core scope of the project.

While the design team is developing wireframes for the initial UX, the build squad needs to come together for an initial meeting, which we call an inception workshop. In this meeting, the build squad reviews its selected approach to remind team members of what practices they will be using, as well as to walk through the MVP and whatever low-fidelity wireframes the designers have developed. The most important part of this process is breaking the MVP definition into small user stories, each of which can be implemented within about a day by a pair of developers. A good user story should be phrased in the context of a persona, describing what that persona experiences while interacting with the system, with well-defined acceptance criteria to let the developers know when they are done. The developers provide input on the technical complexity of the stories, and the whole team works together to get to the right granularity of stories. The developers provide high-level estimates based on story complexity. Some stories may have to be broken into smaller stories for each story to be able to be implemented within a pair-day.

Working with the squad lead, the product owner must develop and maintain a prioritized story backlog of user stories with details for developers to estimate and get started coding with. Here we see an important distinction between the product owner and squad lead job roles. The product owner determines what gets built; the development team (led by the squad lead) determines how it gets built.

Starting Development

We recommend that teams establish a pattern of iterations lasting about one week. We have found that a week is the right length of time for an iteration; it allows a team to accomplish enough to show tangible results, but it does not let the team get too far in the wrong direction before receiving feedback from sponsor users, who let the team know whether a pivot is needed.

Each iteration begins with an iteration planning meeting. In that meeting, the squad lead and product owner make sure that everyone understands the user stories, and the developers perform implementation estimates on each story. The focus is not on the entire backlog, but on the stories that can be implemented within the week. As a result of estimates and feedback gathered from stakeholders and sponsor users, the product manager frequently changes user stories and prioritization of the story backlog. He has full control of what gets developed and can make changes whenever he wants, even in the middle of a story.

As mentioned in the section on our approach to project inception, a key measurement for a user story is that a single development pair should be able to implement it in a single day. The team's implementation velocity can change over time, which may adjust the sizes of stories; stories may be broken up and added back to the backlog or combined. The team makes these adjustments during a daily stand-up meeting in which team members share progress, each pair selects stories from the top of the backlog to work on that day, and each pair shares information on changes in story-size estimates that they need to make as they proceed.

The teams must also follow the practice of Test Driven Design (TDD), which requires developers to write their tests before they write the code being tested. TDD is an important element for making sure that any member of a squad can understand the code — if the developer can read a suite of functional tests they can understand how a particular code element is implemented. The test suite developed through this process should encompass all the major forms of testing that are required: functional, user interface, and performance. As you continue development, you will find that different test suites run at different cadences. You see more performance testing later in the development of the application than earlier in the development cycle, for example. You need to fully embrace automated testing to make TDD viable; automated testing markedly reduces the time that manual tests take.

One of the most distinctive practices that we have adopted as part of the IBM Cloud Garage Method is pair programming. Pair programming has demonstrated a distinct set of advantages to our clients. The first advantage is that when pairs write all code, the code undergoes continuous code review, making it possible to reduce or eliminate time spent on formal code review. Pair programming also increases the focus of your team. You know that your pairs will be working directly on the problem at hand, because it's harder to be distracted by technology while you are interacting directly with another person. By rotating programming pairs daily, you spread the knowledge of individual system elements across the members of a pair and across the entire squad, as pairs implement new user stories and read, revisit, and revise existing code. This practice reduces dependence on any single member of your team, which is called improving the truck number of a team. (If any person were hit by a truck, development would not grind to a halt because that person was a knowledge bottleneck.)

Pair rotation in combination with TDD makes it possible for any team member to participate in a pair with confidence that she knows that it's hard, if not impossible, to break something that she doesn't understand in such a way that it can't be easily rolled back or repaired. This process builds the kind of full-stack developers we discussed in Chapter 4, improving the overall efficiency of your teams by eliminating handoffs to other teams or to specialists with unique skills.

It is important to regularly garner feedback from sponsor users and product owners to make sure that the team is heading in the right direction and can make changes as needed. That's why we insist on weekly demonstrations or playbacks of the iteration results with these stakeholders. Finally, at the end of every iteration, the team gathers for a retrospective, which allows the team to continuously improve its culture and experience.

Figure 8-5 shows how user stories, stand-up meetings, retrospectives, and validation work together.

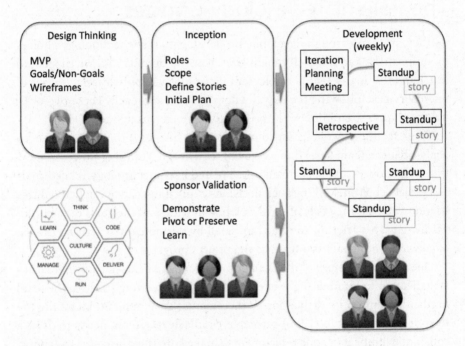

Figure 8-5: Garage Method iteration cycle.

In the first iteration, one of the most important tasks for a new squad is to develop an automated delivery pipeline that automatically builds the code, runs the test suites, report status, and (based on success) deploys through multiple environments to staging. The team may choose to include a manual step in the delivery process to empower the product manager to decide when code should be released to production. It is important for the team to practice continuous integration to feed the delivery pipeline and to make sure that each pair's code doesn't diverge too far from the rest of the team's code. We provide more information on continuous integration and continuous delivery in Chapter 10.

The right set of tools for the Cloud can be enormously helpful in getting a team started quickly. The IBM Cloud Continuous Delivery Service, for example, allows you to define template tool chains that teams can start with and then customize to meet their needs. If a team is implementing a microservices-based application using Cloud Foundry, it could pick a template matching that pattern. You can accomplish the same ends with other tools such as Jenkins, but getting to the same starting point takes more work.

The Role of Technology Choices

As they proceed through development, developers make technology choices to support the rapid development they want to achieve. As we discussed in Chapter 5, many teams implement cloud-native applications as a set of microservices, following the polyglot development approach. These two technology choices are in line with the benefits offered through the Cloud.

These technology choices also need to be in line with the goals (and nongoals) that the team agreed to as part of the Design Thinking process. Many times, developers add goals to an unexpressed list of technology-related goals as a project goes on. Making such decisions explicit instead of implicit reduces friction between the goals of the development team and the goals of the product owner. This friction can be eliminated by periodically revisiting the list of goals and nongoals as a team as the project progresses.

One important aspect of the Lean development and Lean startup approaches is dedication to eliminating waste. Throughout the coding process, the team needs to maintain its dedication to incremental development, including the Keep It Simple, Stupid (KISS) principle. Similarly, the team needs to drive a constant drumbeat of code refactoring to make sure that the code is as simple as it can be yet does not repeat itself needlessly or implement functions that are not yet needed for the current user stories.

Expanding to Deliver the MVP

As the team starts gets closer to delivering the MVP into production, additional practices related to delivery and operations become important. In the process of moving closer to production, tension sometimes arises between the product owner and the squad lead. This tension emerges over user stories about nonfunctional aspects. User stories about availability are just one type of user stories that you need to include in every system. Security is just as important and often overlooked. Discussions of security may even lead to the development of new personas (such as hackers or black hats) that need to be introduced into the persona-mapping process and have stories defined about them.

Also, don't forget operational considerations. Make sure that you count both external personas and internal personas. Include personas such as first responder (see Chapter 10), which could result in nonfunctional user stories about logging, alerting, and dashboarding.

A critical process point that we have to make here is that you must write these user stories as part of the process, but you cannot let these user stories be prioritized so far down the backlog that they are never addressed. A key responsibility of the squad lead in the Garage Method is to make sure that nonfunctional aspects of the application are addressed in addition to the functional aspects. Product owners who think in functional terms first need to be educated in nonfunctional thinking, and they may need to be persuaded that nonfunctional user stories are just as important to the business as functional user stories. You never want to have product owners find themselves not understanding the ramifications of their decisions; for instance, that if you only deploy into one cloud region that they are at risk for the entire application going down in case of the loss of that region for any reason.

In the IBM Cloud Garage Method, this persuasion is part of an ongoing negotiation between the squad lead and the product owner to make sure that the backlog doesn't swing too far in one direction or the other. How critical these nonfunctional requirements are depends on the application and on the team's stage of development.

As the team continues to move more features to production, higher levels of scale, resiliency, and availability are needed, especially when the new site is to replace an existing website. We encourage teams to analyze performance data through automated monitoring to understand resource use. Scaling on the cloud can be addressed through cloud autoscaling services such as the IBM Cloud Autoscaling service and production-level service plans or the autoscaling capability built into Kubernetes. The choice of a microservices architecture, which results in many small, stateless services, can make autoscaling possible. To achieve maximum availability and eliminate the need for disaster recovery, each application should be deployed to multiple cloud data centers in different regions, and data should be replicated across those data centers.

The Role of Testing in the Squad Model

It is worth noting that in the large-scale case, the combination of automated testing, TDD, and pair programming changes an implicit assumption that development teams usually work under: that a large, dedicated staff of testers must be embedded in the teams as part of the development process. The skills of existing quality-assurance staff members still have a place in the process, although there is much less of a need for a dedicated testing role due to the combination of automation and TDD. As a result, there are many fewer dedicated testers needed in the organization, so people will need to find other roles. Some testers may become developers, while others will find that their deep domain knowledge makes them better-suited to be product owners.

An important question that teams often ask when building development pipelines for microservices is what kinds of testing tools they will need. In general, teams have a lot of flexibility, but they need at least three classes of tools:

- Unit testing tools of the xUnit variety, which are common in the early stages of pipelines.
- Graphic user interface (GUI) and acceptance testing tools such as Cucumber, Selenium, and Fitnesse, which allow you to specify what the end-user experience and end-to-end interactions look like. These tools can include integration with cloud-based tools such as Sauce Labs.
- Performance testing tools (usually based on something like Jmeter), which may be on-premises or cloud-based.

Security testing is also critical. As we discussed in Chapter 6, every DevOps pipeline should include tools that check for static and dynamic vulnerabilities. Later, more active tests such as penetration tests also become necessary.

Usually, large enterprises still need a small, specialized end-to-end testing squad to perform types of tests that require specialized skills — in particular, cross-device mobile testing and end-to-end performance testing. Commonly, to avoid handoffs, the experts in those unique areas are temporarily added to build squads as needed.

Customer Example

At a large airline, one of the most important constituencies to persuade about the applicability of the IBM Cloud Garage Method was the architect community. As we worked with the airline on cloud adoption, we realized that we had to make some customizations in the IBM Cloud Garage Method to meet the needs of this community. This taught us that a support squad was needed around architecture.

We designated a special support squad consisting of the application architects and a few specialist architect roles, sometimes including a test architect and one or more systems architects. The members of that squad split their time among the build squads, sometimes advising them on the ramifications of implementation decisions within the guidance set up at the project level, but more often simply helping with the kind of architecture planning that has to happen at the epic and sprint levels.

The first application to go live using the IBM Cloud Garage Method was Reaccommodation. The Reaccommodation app aimed to relieve the biggest frustrations of flying: flight delays and cancellations. The app fundamentally changed passengers' experience by giving them full control of flight rebooking by using the mobile or web application. With Reaccommodation, passengers have the flexibility to choose flight options, including alternative schedules, stops, and connections, which has significantly shortened wait times for passengers and reduced the workload of support-staff members, call-center personnel, and gate attendants and demonstrated the success of the application of the method at scale. The application allows customers to view and accept new flights and shop for other flights during irregular operations, which dramatically decreased the number of calls and improved the customer experience.

Using the Garage Method, the customer team partnered with IBM to develop the application, using practices such as pair programming and TDD. The result was a first-of-a-kind cloud-native application built on a microservices architecture with a modern web interface and responsive design. The project was a major win for IBM and served as a role model for subsequent projects with the customer.

The team enthusiastically took to iteration planning and pair programming; it found that pairing enabled knowledge transfer and collaboration and reduced stress as the burden of implementing a user story was distributed between the members of a pair. The team also enjoyed its ability to reorder, add, and resize stories as development progressed, as well as the productive, collaborative atmosphere that the method created.

This project was completed in half the time that the customer expected, from inception to initial launch in a bit less than four months. The business has become so comfortable and confident with this approach that when Hurricane Irma caused widespread disruption, the airline accelerated the Reaccommodation rollout to allow more airports to be serviced by the application.

Nonetheless, although the project was a huge success, we felt that some things could have been done differently. The biggest issue with this project was that Squad leads and the IBM Cloud Garage method were dropped onto an existing team. As a result, we didn't get the chance to show the team how to apply Design Thinking to the extent that we wanted to, because the team had completed screen design before the IBM team engaged. Some minor issues could have been resolved by earlier customer feedback, even by using low-fidelity paper mockups and storyboards. Also, because the team was an existing team, we couldn't right-size it to the ten-person limit of a normal squad. Simply having more people than the preferred size meant that the team lost some ability to react quickly because of additional communication paths. In other words, we couldn't change direction as quickly as we wanted to.

Summary

In this chapter, we've taken you through a whirlwind tour of the IBM Cloud Garage Method. We highlighted the practices of the IBM Design Thinking, Lean startup, and Agile methods that make up the IBM Cloud Garage Method. More important. we showed you how these practices come together and why we chose them to fit together into a cohesive whole.

In the next chapter, we introduce the final piece of our methodological puzzle: involving your operations team (at the squad level and at a more global level) in your Cloud adoption journey by introducing ideas from DevOps and site reliability engineering.

9

Service Management and Operations

Independent of where applications run — in traditional IT data centers or in the cloud — they must be managed to ensure availability, security, and adequate quality of service for the users of the applications.

Service Management and Operations is the discipline that designs, delivers, and manages the functions necessary to use information technology within an organization. Service Management is a mature and well-defined function, often aligned with the de facto industry standard IT infrastructure library (ITIL).

And here lies the problem: How can a process-heavy, mature operations team evolve to support modern Agile and cloud-oriented approaches? This is what we will discuss in this chapter.

What Does Cloud Mean for the VP of Operations?

Operations is a well-defined discipline with many years of experience manifested by organization, processes, and tools. As applications and workload move to the cloud, the established service management and operations processes must be revisited. The goal must be to reach a balance among service reliability, higher velocity, and productivity to respond more quickly to market opportunities and threats. If you don't reach a balance between both positions, the result will be conflict among departments, often paired with distrust.

The issue is that traditional IT service management (ITSM) processes are perceived as being cumbersome, complex, and in conflict with practices such as Agile and DevOps. This perception results in solutions being built and used inside organizations without explicit approval — a situation sometimes called Shadow IT. Unfortunately, Shadow IT can lead to compliance issues, inefficiencies, and organizational dysfunction.

Cloud adoption can be an opportunity to revisit and renew established ITSM practices. As you will see in this chapter, this opportunity affects culture, organizations, roles, processes, tools, and technology. We believe that a modern cloud-oriented service management practice can support and extend the business value gained through Agile methodologies and DevOps.

Most companies consume services from more than one cloud. If the adoption of new practices is not enough of a challenge, synchronizing across multiple providers certainly is. Service integration and management (SIAM) supports the delivery of an end-to-end integrated service experience to your clients and spans providers in internal and external business units.

A key to achieving balance is a well-thought-out definition of the services and the underlying service-level agreement (SLA) or at least the service-level objective (SLO) offered to the users of the service. The SLA enables all departments (business, development, and operations) to rally behind a common goal and acts as the base for decisions. This alignment enables the vice president of operations to fulfill his or her role as a strategic partner of the business while executing his or her obligations of governance and stewardship.

Operational Transformation

Cloud service management and operations (CSMO) redefines traditional service management to better fit the need for cloud while bridging to traditional approaches to service management, such as the IT infrastructure library (ITIL).

Service management encompasses all the operational aspects of applications and services. After an application is pushed to production, it must be managed, which includes monitoring to ensure availability and performance according to SLAs and SLOs. This management also includes aspects such as capacity management, compliance, resiliency, and scalability.

As methods of developing, testing, and releasing new functions become more agile, service management must transform to support this paradigm shift. The transformation has implications in various areas:

- **Organization:** Instead of having operations be distant from the development team, full life-cycle responsibility is provided through small teams called squads. Site reliability engineering (SRE) brings a strong engineering focus to operations. SRE emphasizes automation and prevention to scale operations as load increases.
- **Process:** Automated and continuous testing, deployment, and release of functions are key elements of DevOps. Existing service management processes, such as change management processes, must change to support this approach.
- **Technology:** Because time is of the essence in restoring a service, incident management tools must provide rapid access to the right information, support automation, and instant collaboration with subject-matter experts (SMEs). As an example of a technology transformation, we introduce a new collaborative technique called ChatOps that improves the ability of teams to respond quickly to incidents. We also address how chatbot technology integrates with service management and DevOps tools as part of this collaboration.
- **Culture:** As in any transformation project, you must consider a few cultural aspects to be successful. One example is the need for a culture of blameless postmortems in which an organization can learn from the cause of an incident without pointing fingers. Also, a culture of transparency is essential to cloud-oriented operations.

Organizational changes

In traditional IT, many companies have well-defined development and operations organizations. The development department is responsible for developing and testing code; it can be characterized by a thirst for new features, velocity, and productivity. This department works on projects. The operations department is responsible for maintaining and operating applications; it can be characterized by focus on stability, performance, reliability, and correctness. This department works on products.

This setup creates natural conflict between these organizations, frequently leading to distrust. People in the two organizations have different backgrounds, skills, and incentives.

DevOps is a software engineering practice that aims to unify software development (Dev) and software operation (Ops), which obviously affects the organizational structure.

DevOps

DevOps builds a working relationship between the operations and development teams. In an ideal case, development teams (squads) are responsible for the entire life cycle of the application, from planning, building, testing, and deployment to the release, run, and operation stages. Supporting this cycle requires removing the organizational boundaries between development and operations. Team members share goals and seek a healthy balance between velocity and stability.

Staffing DevOps with people who have the right skills presents a challenge. In an ideal case, every team member can assume every other team member's role. Frequently, however, team members have particular specialties. Some members are development- or test-focused; others are deployment- or operations-focused. In any case, you want to cross-pollinate skills so that members gain secondary specialties in addition to their primary roles on the team.

Figure 9-1 shows the evolution from a traditional siloed IT organization towards an integrated organization, where teams become responsible end-to-end for the entire lifecycle of the service.

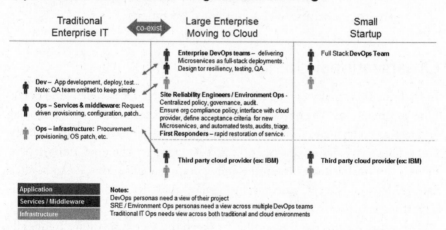

Figure 9-1: Organizational change.

Although the DevOps squad approach has a lot of advantages, it falls short in certain operational activities that affect multiple DevOps teams. Modern operations require broad and deep skills across multiple technology domains. Not every DevOps team member, however, is skilled enough to build an efficient automation approach or a scalable, distributed log management solution. Also, if each squad retains the ability to make its own technical decisions on tools and platform, you optimize for individual components but fail to optimize for the entire system. The result is a lack of synergy and efficiency, as well as challenges to members' ability to join different squads.

The DevOps approach does not apply when the following conditions exist:

- Applications are built with a commercial-off-the-shelf product that needs to be operated
- Applications are in maintenance mode, in which no new functional development is taking place, but the application still must be operated and maintained
- The number of operational tasks that software engineers want to do is culturally limited

One way to address these challenges is to retain a small number of operations experts to form one or more operations squads. These squads are responsible for the design, development, and delivery of operational products used by development squads. You must set up parallel governance aspects to police development squads' ability to make operational decisions.

Site reliability engineering

Another approach to operations is site reliability engineering. According to Ben Treynor, founder of Google's site reliability team, SRE is "what happens when a software engineer is tasked with what used to be called operations."[1]

SRE enables operations to proceed at the velocity of modern development teams. Site reliability engineers write automation to efficiently perform operational tasks, eliminating manual toil. They are on call for up to 50 percent of the time to understand where automation could be most effective. They spend the other 50 percent of their time improving the environment. Excess operational load flows from the SRE team to the development team, which automatically slows velocity in favor of stability. Another 5 percent of the operational activity is shared with the development team, so that site reliability engineers are continually reminded of the operational characteristics of their application or service.

SRE prevents issues from reoccurring. Instead of just responding to an incident more quickly, site reliability engineers put their energy into preventing incidents. They address the causes of incidents to improve nonfunctional aspects of the environment, architecture, and applications. Site reliability engineers are empowered to perform code changes themselves; they don't necessarily depend on developers to implement backlog items.

A key metric is an agreed-upon SLO that drives priorities. If the SLO is met, velocity may increase, and the team can be more aggressive in adding features and rolling out new releases. If the SLO is about to be missed, velocity is slowed in favor of stability and improvements in service reliability. The currency used is an error budget, which is the maximum allowable threshold for errors and outages.

DevOps and SRE complement each other nicely. The DevOps methodology makes robust code a goal for each member of the development squad. Rather than throwing the code over the wall to the operations team, developers have an intrinsic interest in the reliability of their service. The SRE approach enables operations to scale through automation and balance new features with the need to reduce technical debt. The result is operational efficiency across the entire organization.

A combination of DevOps and SRE is also useful when separation of duties is required, such as in highly regulated environments. This approach requires adoption of a converged model that combines the values of both approaches.

Process changes

Cloud enables many activities to be automated. Environments are automatically provisioned, applications are automatically deployed, and application instances are automatically scaled up or down based on policies, which affects operational processes. What were once manual steps should be automated and integrated into the delivery pipeline.

Consider change management. In traditional IT, changes and releases are performed manually. The change advisory board (CAB) assesses each change and approves it for implementation in the next stage in the development life cycle. The change is scheduled for implementation in the forward schedule of changes (FSC).

CONTINUOUS DELIVERY

Continuous delivery (CD) gets changes of all types — including new features, configuration changes, bug fixes, and experiments — into production or into the hands of users as safely and quickly as sustainable.

CD requires that code changes flow constantly from development all the way through to production. To continuously deliver in a consistent, reliable way, a team must break the software delivery process into delivery stages and automate the movement of the code through the stages to create a delivery pipeline.

In a cloud-native environment — characterized by continuous integration/continuous delivery (CI/CD) — a change is automatically promoted through the various stages. Assessments previously performed by the CAB, such as validating successful test execution, are now performed automatically. In ITIL terms, preapproved changes or standard changes become the norm. Change is implemented instantaneously, without the need for an artificial FSC that slows velocity. Release to production is performed thoughtfully through strategies such as canary releases, in which the deployment is initially performed to a subset called the canary. If canary deployment is successful, full deployment is performed. Related techniques such as blue-green deployment allow immediate rollback in case an error is identified in production.

The role of the CAB shifts from assessing individual changes to the definition of the delivery pipeline and its policies, including answering questions such as "How much code coverage is required for a test stage to declare a test as sufficient?" and "What is the subset acting as the canary for the deployment?"

Figure 9-2 shows the evolution of processes from traditional IT towards cloud-oriented and cloud-native environments:

Technology changes

Like roles and processes, technology changes as workloads move to the cloud. Although most of these changes are independent of the cloud, cloud adoption has a significant influence on the adoption of new tools and technologies.

Operations Transformation – Processes Change

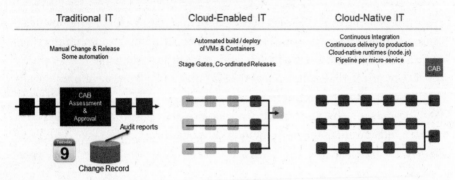

Figure 9-2: Process change.

Monitoring tools, for example, need to be able to observe new workloads. The focus shifts from resource-centric monitoring (file system, processes, memory) to application- and service-oriented monitoring (response time, latency, error rate, saturation). Going hand in hand with this shift in perspective is the need to make metric data available in dashboards. In the past, many monitoring tools generated an alert only to notify the SysAdmin about a threshold being breached. The metric distribution over time or a comparison with other metrics was not made available to the SysAdmin.

Two more areas where technology changes have influenced the approach to operations is in the introduction of ChatOps and the emergence of new ways to manage backlogs of action items.

ChatOps

One of the most disruptive technology changes is ChatOps, which describes a shift toward a more collaborative way to perform operations. Rather than communicating through incident records (tickets) and phone calls, SMEs (DevOps team members, security experts, or network experts) use instant-messaging tools to communicate about incidents with one another and with tools.

In the past, operations teams wasted time by creating tickets and documenting updates through ticket changes. Because this process was so cumbersome, a lot of important information was not tracked through tickets. Instead, people found alternative ways of communicating more directly, such as email, Skype, Sametime, or WhatsApp.

ChatOps recognizes the need for instant, direct collaboration among SMEs. Tools such as Slack and Hipchat provide instant group messaging. In addition to text messages, media (such as a screen shot) or files (such as a configuration file or the output of a command) can be shared. These tools store messages persistently, so people joining the conversation later have access to all previous communications.

Although instant, collaborative communication among humans is already very attractive, ChatOps allows systems to participate in the conversation as well. ITSM and DevOps tools send information such as event notifications directly to the group chats. Examples include showing related events or reporting response-time distribution over the past 24 hours.

Using chatbot technology, these tools can listen to the communication and react to certain messages by responding to commands. Scripts can reply to requests for information about the most recent deployment performed, providing a list of code changes and the name of the submitter.

Using the example of ChatOps, Figure 9-3 shows the evolution of technology from traditional service management tools towards more collaborative and cloud-oriented tools:

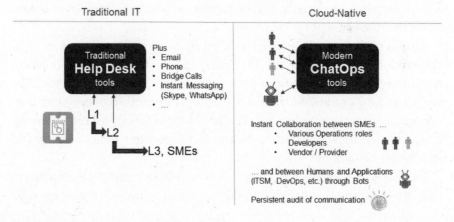

Figure 9-3: Technology changes.

ChatOps can be applied to various disciplines of service management:

- **Incident management:** ChatOps can perform incident analysis, isolation, and investigation, especially when people join the process over time and need to be onboarded quickly.
- **Root-cause analysis (RCA)/problem management:** ChatOps can be applied to perform the 5 Whys technique. It could further be leveraged to develop and prioritize a balanced action plan. See the section in this chapter on "Root-Cause Analysis and Postmortems" for more information.
- **Change management:** ChatOps can be applied to conduct a virtual change advisory board to perform change impact assessment and schedule the implementation of a change to the application.

ChatOps enables collaborative communication among humans and ITSM/DevOps tools, reducing incident response time, eliminating repetitive requests for information by humans, and ensuring that every DevOps team member has consistent access to the incident information that he needs.

Even with ChatOps technologies, traditional help-desk ticketing systems may still play a role. Incident start and end times, as well as major updates, may still be propagated (automatically) to the help-desk ticketing tools.

Backlog

Another example where new technology is applied is in the area of handling action items as a result of an incident and the corresponding root cause analysis. Actions focus on different elements of the lifecycle, such as restorative actions address a quick restoration of the service, whereas preventative actions tackle the root cause of the incident.

Actions resulting from these operational phases are no longer kept in isolation inside the Operations team. They are rather shared with the development teams and combined with any feature requirements in a common backlog. The merged backlog enables the team to make proper prioritization decisions, considering the functional requirements as well as non-functional requirements. It becomes a critical element for the product owner to balance velocity and stability for his product.

Technologies such as electronic Kanban-Boards help gaining the necessary visibility of all requests against, allowing the squad teams performing the right decisions. It also allows an objective measurement of the technical debt and the burn-rate of any actions related to the reliability of the solution.

Cultural changes

Another element supports all the other transformation initiatives: culture. Traditional IT service management is characterized by a precisely defined and structured approach, which is often in conflict with an Agile and iterative development approach that tolerates failure as a way to learn.

We are not implying that teams need to accept outages as part of the new way of doing business. In fact, resiliency is a key element of a cloud-oriented approach to service management. In the following sections, we examine the cultural elements that enable this approach.

Figure 9-4 shows the cultural differences between Traditional IT and a Cloud-native approach.

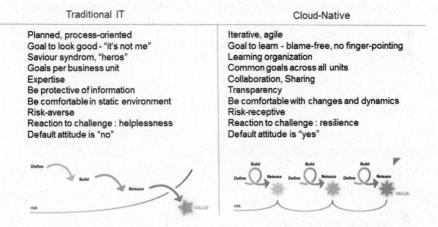

Figure 9-4: Cultural changes.

Blameless RCA

As you see later in this chapter, blameless RCA is critical. The goal is not only to find out what happened, but also discover how to improve the way that the organization responds. You want to create an environment in which team members share lessons learned to help prevent others from making the same mistakes. To create that environment, you first have to address any disincentives, such as fear of punishment or reprimands.

Transparency

Another critical cultural aspect is transparency. Creating trust across virtual teams dissolves the boundaries between them. Here are a few areas in which transparency should be applied:

- **Code:** Access to the source code (including a daily submission to the code repository) is granted to everyone in the company.
- **Backlog:** Access to functional and nonfunctional requirements and prioritization is granted to everyone in the company. Providing details on the decision-making process help you get support from members of the affected community.
- **Metrics:** Availability and metric data is made available to internal and external consumers of the services.
- **Incident investigation and problem management:** What happened in the incident and the lessons learned from it are documented and made available so that the organization benefits from the experience. An example is open access to all RCAs.

Engineering-oriented approach to operations

SRE is an engineering-oriented approach to operations that uses rigid engineering practices to solve hard problems. The operations culture needs to transition from trial and error to an engineering approach by following the scientific method:

1. Develop a hypothesis.
2. Plan the activity.
3. Evaluate the result.
4. Learn/iterate.

Another aspect is to make data-driven decisions characterized by elements such as an error budget, prioritization of incidents by SLA (or affected users), and prioritization of backlog items.

Cultural change is hard, and it's complicated by the fact that it happens within the strictures of an organization. Although you and your squad may understand the new cultural values, outsiders who have control of budgets or approvals may not see things the same way.

One way to support a cultural transformation is to clearly articulate core values. Ideally, these values are developed from the bottom up, such as through a brainstorming jam.[2] After the values are defined, they need to be endorsed and supported throughout leadership, starting with the highest level possible (such as chief executive or chief technology officer).

New Roles

Transitioning to a cloud-oriented service management solution can be quite disruptive. A good starting point for the transformation is looking at changes in roles and responsibilities and in the organizational structure.

Roles and responsibilities

When you move toward adopting the cloud, certain activities are no longer required, because the service provider handles those tasks. In a Platform as a Service (PaaS) environment, for example, the installation and maintenance of a database is performed by the PaaS provider. Another characteristic is that many operational activities are automated to meet high availability and reliability needs in a cost-effective way.

Although some activities are no longer required, the remaining activities are performed in a slightly different and more Agile way. We describe a few of these changing roles in the following sections.

First responder

One critical requirement is service availability, which means that a service needs to be restored as quickly as possible. In a traditional environment, time is wasted in handoffs. A level-1 team creates a ticket; a level-2 team performs triage and diagnostic actions; yet another team of platform engineers performs service restoration.

In the new model, a team of first responders assumes the activities of level-1, level-2, and platform engineers. Team members are skilled and empowered to perform initial triage, isolation, and restoration of the service. Only if the team is not able to restore the service are additional experts pulled into the incident management process.

Incident commander

In case first responders are not able to resolve an incident, an incident commander is assigned to ensure effective handling and communication of the incident. This person's job is the proper management of incident diagnosis and resolution.

The incident commander pulls in additional resources and subject-matter expertise as needed. At the same time, she communicates status with affected parties, stakeholders, and (most important) end users. Transparency about ongoing progress is critical for gaining and maintaining trust.

When service is restored and the incident is closed, the incident commander leads RCA and conducts a postmortem review of the incident. Because the incident commander was at the center of the incident resolution, she can best drive the answers to the 5 Whys (see the section later in this chapter, "Root-Cause Analysis and Postmortems").

Site reliability engineer

As the number of applications and/or users increases, you could throw more people at the problem, but this solution is not scalable. Rather, you need an operational model that scales effectively (i.e., less than linear) with the amount of load and dynamics of the workload. Ideally, administrators want to engineer themselves out of the problem.

A very effective method used for this purpose is SRE. Site reliability engineers write automation to efficiently perform operational tasks and eliminate manual toil. They improve the nonfunctional aspects of the environment, architecture, and applications to address the root-cause of the incident. SREs are frequently a mix of systems administrators and developers — some companies only hire developers into the role. Site reliability engineers need to be able to work hand in hand with developers to improve the code.

Site reliability engineers take an end-to-end view of an application. They are not just subject-matter experts for one tower (system, network, database) or component (microservice). Site reliability engineers are system thinkers who take a holistic view of an application and its interdependencies, which is especially important for dealing with performance- and capacity-related issues.

Availability manager

The availability manager is responsible for overall service. She negotiates the SLA and/or the underlying SLO.

Together with the DevOps engineers, she defines the release strategy for the service, which could include blue-green deployment and canary testing; she also defines when to roll back or roll forward. The availability manager participates in development practices such as stand-ups and retrospectives.

The availability manager collaborates with the site reliability engineers and incident commanders in applying error budgets to control change velocity. She also participates in RCA and postmortem activities to develop a balanced action plan and to make sure that nonfunctional requirements resulting from the RCA are prioritized accordingly in the development backlog.

Additional roles

In addition to the key roles we described above, a cloud-oriented operations team may have many more roles, such as these:

- DevOps engineer
- ChatOps developer
- Automation analyst
- Dashboard designer and developer
- Continued service improvement analyst
- Artificial intelligence/machine learning/cognitive analyst
- Cloud operator

Organizational alignment

After you define new roles, you need to define how they fit into your organizational structure. In previous chapters, we discussed the model of squads and tribes. In this section, we show you how to align the development team with the operations team in this model.

In the first iteration of DevOps, you want the squads to be self-sufficient and have end-to-end responsibility for the entire life cycle of the application or service. This model counters the previous approach of throwing the code over the wall to the operations team by making it a goal of developers to write robust code. Figure 9-5 shows multiple DevOps teams that are responsible for the full lifecycle of their application.

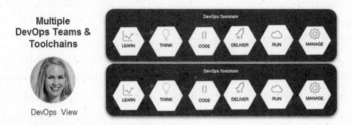

Figure 9-5: DevOps squad model.

Although this approach is certainly a good start on DevOps, it requires each squad member to be an expert not only on the development front, but also on operational activities. Not every DevOps team is skilled enough to build a comprehensive service management solution, however, and this fact is amplified as more squads are formed. Even if the team has the right expertise, due to the autonomy of squads, teams may not learn from one another.

Introducing a central operations squad may help. This squad provides consulting and assistance for the DevOps teams. It also provides central services for capabilities that are hard to set up and maintain or that serve multiple teams (such as a central log or event management solution or an automation backbone). Figure 9-6 shows the linkage of multiple DevOps teams and a central operational squad.

This model is not a step back to the traditional model of development and operations, but a converged model that acknowledges and leverages the autonomy of the DevOps squads while providing efficiency of scale for some shared functions.

Adding SRE further enhances this model. At least one SRE squad is dedicated to operational services offered to the DevOps community; site reliability engineers in these squads own these services end to end. Examples of these services are automation framework, self-service infrastructure, logging and metrics, and operational scorecard.

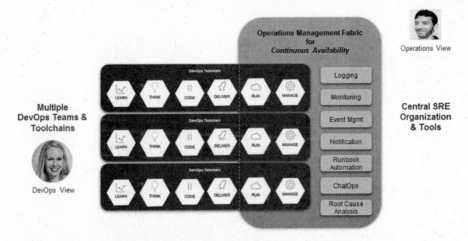

Figure 9-6: DevOps squad model with operational squad.

In addition, each DevOps squad contains site reliability engineers, who focus on the nonfunctional aspects of the service or application for which the squad is responsible. Rather than aligning by operational function, they align by application. Examples of their responsibilities could include high availability, rate limiting, zero-downtime deployment, performance, resiliency, and serviceability.

Figure 9-7 shows this enhanced model with a central SRE organization as well as SREs as members in each of the DevOps squads.

The number of site reliability engineers per DevOps squad depends on the health and quality of the services, indicated by aspects such as the operational scorecard (see the section, "Operational Readiness," later in this chapter) and the number of backlog items resulting from previous incidents. The site reliability engineers are not simply the operations team within the DevOps squad. The entire DevOps squad is still responsible for the service end to end, and each member is on call to fix defects. The SRE members specialize in nonfunctional aspects; the DevOps members specialize in functional development.

All site reliability engineers — the ones on the SRE squad as well as the ones on the DevOps squads — should be virtually connected. Together, they form an SRE guild as shown in Figure 9-8. In the SRE guild, members share operational experience and insight across the organization.

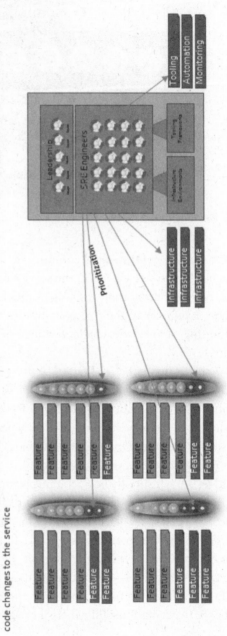

Legend:
SRE
Developer

SRE Squad

- SRE Lead drives org-wide priorities
- Engineers rotate on flexible cadence between SRE and Feature squads (some core remain)

Development Squads

- Levels of maturity drive amount of resource required for SRE backlog
- 90% of the time these team members are the ones making code changes to the service

Figure 9-7: DevOps squad model with SRE squad model.

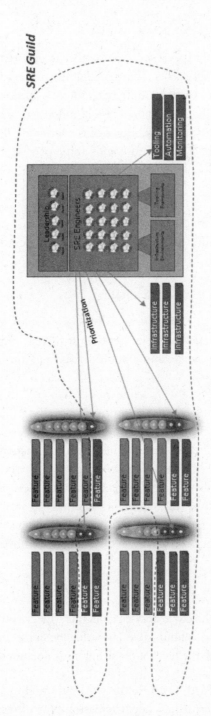

Figure 9-8: SRE guild model.

Operational Readiness

Organizations have to follow a set of guidelines to ensure that they can effectively operate and manage risks. These guidelines are based on common sense as well as experience. Certain industries impose additional guidelines on companies to ensure that operational risk is contained so as to not negatively affect users or the ecosystem. Examples of the latter are Basel-2 and HIPAA.

As companies adopt cloud technologies and move workloads to the cloud, existing guidelines have to be adapted. In this section, we discuss this topic from two viewpoints:

- Is the cloud operationally ready for the company?
- Is the application that's moving to the cloud operationally ready?

Operationalizing the cloud

As a company adopts a new platform, its processes, roles, and responsibilities must be revisited to determine whether they still apply or need to be tailored. The same is true when you adopt a public, dedicated, or private cloud.

Using a RACI matrix

Operationalizing the cloud starts with understanding the roles and responsibilities of the cloud provider and the consumer of these cloud services. We suggest that you define these responsibilities with a responsible, accountable, consulted, and informed (RACI) matrix. In a RACI matrix, you list key activities and map the involvement of various parties to these activities.

Peter Weill and Jeanne Ross, in their book on IT governance, convincingly outline the need for IT governance decision-rights frameworks.[3] A RACI matrix is a common way of implementing a decision-rights framework to clarify roles and responsibilities.

The matrix shows key activities as rows and participating parties as columns. In the first instance, the table would have only two columns: the cloud service provider and the cloud service consumer. Later you can add additional detail by breaking these columns into individual business units or departments. For each resulting cell, the level of involvement is documented as either

- **Responsible:** Parties that do the work required to achieve the task. At least one role must have a participation type of responsible, although others can be delegated to assist in the work required.

■ **Accountable** (also approver or approving authority): The party that is ultimately accountable for the correct, thorough completion of the deliverable or task and delegates the work to the responsible roles. In other words, an accountable must sign off on (approve) work that a responsible provides. Only one accountable is specified for each task or deliverable.

■ **Consulted:** Parties whose opinions are sought (typically, SMEs) and those with whom two-way communication exists.

■ **Informed:** Parties who are kept up to date on progress, often only on the completion of the task or deliverable, and with whom one-way communication exists.

Table 9-1 shows an example of a RACI Matrix. Such RACI Matrices typically contain hundreds of rows, detailing all operational activities to be performed.

Table 9-1 Example RACI Matrix

Area	Use Case	Service Consumer	Service Provider
Private Cloud	Install necessary components (i.e., Helm Charts)	C	R, A
Private Cloud	Connect and integrate monitoring with Backend	C	R, A
Private Cloud	Backup of configuration files	C, I	R, A
Network	Connect and ensure network performance	C	R, A
Security	Perform post-install security checklist	R, A	R
Security	Verify remote access control	R, A	C
Backup	Provide backup sizing needs	C	R, A

Integrating the platform with existing ITSM landscape

You must also consider how to integrate the new platform into the existing ITSM landscape.

A cloud platform typically provides a service catalog listing various services; sometimes, it provides the same service in different qualities. An organization that is implementing a hybrid cloud strategy, for example, could receive multiple disconnected service catalogs. Also, not every service offered by the cloud provider is approved for consumption, for reasons such as cost or compliance. Therefore, one task could be to combine individual service catalogs into a single service catalog. This process also enables central governance tasks such as costing and billing.

A second consideration is the fact that cloud service providers inform their users about planned maintenance or changes and known disruptions of service in various ways. These notifications could be provided on status pages or made available via application programming interfaces (APIs), a Really Simple Syndication (RSS) feed, or even email. Not all notifications are applicable to a given user, so that information needs to be cleansed for relevance. The operations team is not expected to scan and evaluate these notifications; instead, these announcements are ingested and made available to internal systems (event correlation and management systems, incident management tools, dashboards, and so on).

Other aspects of integration may include the following:

- Help-desk systems are integrated with the support systems of the provider.
- CI information from the cloud platform, such as instances and services, are integrated into the existing configuration management database (CMDB).
- Usage and license information from the cloud platform is populated into the existing CMDB.

Operationalizing application readiness

As applications transition to microservices, businesses need to look for guidelines and processes to ensure that these services are robust and serviceable. Several guidelines (such as the Twelve-Factor App manifesto[4]) exist for developers to follow when building modern web-based applications; these guidelines can be viewed as best practices for creating microservices. There has been little discussion of what it means to build production-ready microservices, however. This discussion must go beyond technical questions to organizational, process, and cultural elements. Unless developers have a vested interest in building high-quality, robust services, they tend to fall back on old habits, in particular favoring new functionality over operational (nonfunctional) aspects. Meeting the production needs of a service — security, compliance, resilience, availability, performance, and so on — requires not only the right technical implementation, but also a high-performing organization and Agile, integrated processes.

Even if DevOps is implemented across the organization with teams that have end-to-end responsibility, you need to govern at scale across the organization.

New operating models such as SRE can become key enablers of an efficient operating culture. But unless development teams have to adhere to well-defined rules, even SRE organizations will be less efficient in operating a cloud-enabled landscape at scale.

You must define, communicate, and enforce clear guidelines to address these shortcomings. These guidelines help assess whether a microservice or other cloud service is high-quality and operationally ready. Your DevOps pipeline should automatically check these guidelines to remove any ambiguity about interpreting them and store the results. Then you can weigh the results by relevance, aggregate them into an overall score, and publish that score on scorecards and dashboards.

Here are some examples of technical guidelines:

- Implement a HealthCheck API to expose the health of the service.
- Ensure that the service is stateless so that it can scale horizontally.
- Ensure that services don't use any local files (such as log and configuration files).
- Ensure that the latest versions of libraries are used (version currency).
- Make topology information available (in a dependency and topology database, for example).
- Provide first-failure data capture to expedite rapid incident resolution.

Following are some examples of nontechnical guidelines and approaches:

- The service owner (product manager) is defined.
- The SRE team responsible for operating the service is defined.
- Runbooks are provided that describe mitigation actions for known cases.
- Service documentation (such as architecture, key metrics, configuration, and tuning guidelines) is made available.
- Chaotic testing is implemented to ensure the resiliency of individual services and applications.
- Regular validation of backup and restore capability is performed.
- Deployment cadence is documented.
- Rack diversity is specified.

If a service fails to comply with the rules within the service contract, repercussions will result. At the same time, there should be direct incentives for adhering to the rules. This pain-and-gain approach (also known as "carrot-and-stick") has shown positive effects in several organizations.

Incident Management

Users have high expectations of availability and performance, so dealing with disruptions in service (incidents) is critical. This task isn't only the job of the operations team in modern cloud-enabled or cloud-native environments; developers and architects also contribute to make their applications robust. This approach is partly based on the evolution of application architectures and best practices. In addition, the DevOps approach, in which the development team is responsible for the entire life cycle of the application, makes robustness an explicit developer goal.

Designing resilient applications for the cloud

Architects and developers acknowledge the need for robustness and have created practices to build inherently resilient applications. A few of these emerging practices are

- **Designing applications for high availability:** Each component of the application is served by multiple active instances residing in different availability zones. A load balancer in front of the application distributes load across multiple instances. In the case of an instance outage, the load balancer simply redirects the traffic to another instance.
- **Enabling scalability of the application based on policy:** When load increases, additional instances are provisioned automatically and removed if the load decreases.
- **Implementing near-zero-downtime deployments via a blue-green deployment strategy:** New versions of the application are deployed without affecting the current releases. When ready, the load balancer redirects traffic to the new version. This practice also provides a convenient approach for rollback, configuring the load balancer toward the previous version of the application.
- **Implementing graceful degradation of a service in case of a dependency failure.** So-called Circuit Breakers[5] allow user code to check if external dependencies are available before actually connecting to the external system. If they detect a malfunctioning downstream service, they avoid trying to call it and find a graceful mitigation.

With all these changes, do you still need traditional incident management? You certainly do! These architectural patterns make incidents less likely, but they still happen. In addition to availability issues, bottlenecks on latency, performance, and capacity are sources of incidents.

Taking a fresh approach to incident management

First, we'll define the scope of incident management: the ability to restore a service as quickly as possible and to minimize the effect on the users of the service. At this stage, we aren't concerned with the root cause of the incident; we address the cause during the problem management phase. Rather than spending too much time investigating causes, resulting in even more downtime, focus on the restoration of the service. You can accomplish this task in many ways, such as rolling back a change, implementing a workaround, or restarting the service.

In cloud-oriented environments, the distinction between incident and problem management is critical, as availability is central to many SLAs. Interestingly, ITIL shares the same definition of incident management. In this view, cloud-oriented operations are not so different from traditional IT service management.

Next, we identify the capabilities that incident management needs to fulfill its mission. Monitoring, notification, and collaboration make up the basic tool chain of incident management.

Monitoring

Monitoring is a well-established discipline in IT operations. Metric data is gathered and evaluated against thresholds to detect any violation or deviation from the expected behavior. Monitoring tools are typically configured to identify issues before they affect service users. Metrics collected are those that signal availability and performance issues, such as latency and error rate.

Modern monitoring tools apply analytics to detect and predict deviations from normal behavior. These tools observe the system over time and build a baseline against which metric values are compared.

The monitoring system simulates a real user by running synthetic transaction from outside the data center. Although the desire by everyone in Operations is to catch issues before they affect users, users should still be able to report issues, especially functional issues, in which the application is not providing a desired outcome.

Notification

Although dashboards are important for proper visibility into the environment and applications, you can't expect first responders to monitor them constantly for violations. First responders need to be notified about alerts so that they can respond immediately. Notification can occur through various channels, such as email, text messages, and apps.

Because applications are redundant by design (see the previous section on Operational Readiness), notifications take place only if users are affected or about to become affected. Notifications of noncritical alerts should be suppressed until the next business day to keep the on-call process effective.

Notification systems implement escalation policies so that the right SME is notified based on assignment groups and on-call schedule. More sophisticated systems also take the current workload into account. If an SME is already involved in a high-severity incident, she will not be alerted again, which allows her to finish the most important activities and avoid burnout.

Collaboration

To restore the service as quickly as possible, SMEs collaborate closely to identify and resolve the incident. ChatOps, described earlier in this chapter, is critical to many cloud-oriented operations teams.

For high-severity alerts, a dedicated channel is created for SMEs to collaborate on and share relevant information such as command output or configuration-file content. The appropriate SMEs will be invited to join the channel as defined by policies.

In case additional domain expertise is needed, SMEs will be invited to participate in the collaboration. The persistent storage of information is important to ease and expedite the onboarding of new people joining the conversation. Collaboration is enhanced by enabling tools to participate in the conversation. The monitoring tool can provide regular updates to the incident by posting a message, for example.

Whereas ChatOps tools provide features that ease remote collaboration, well-established techniques such as bridge calls and war-room-style gathering of experts can still be used. ChatOps tools complement and support these traditional approaches and can replace them as teams gain more expertise in working with the new processes.

Event management

One common problem with the model in which monitoring directly feeds notification systems is that too many notifications can be generated, resulting in lack of trust in the solution. Alerting on symptoms (rather than effects), redundant information, or noncritical events creates noise in the system.

Event management comes into play in this situation. Before an alert notifies a user, an intelligent system analyzes the alert. The event management system suppresses duplicates, correlates dependent events, and enriches events with meaningful information (such as the affected service, the associated SLA, and a link to expert advice). The result is a well-described, actionable alert that triggers the notification of the right SME who has the right information.

Runbooks

To respond to incidents quickly, SMEs need to know how to respond appropriately to alerts. A learning organization needs to tap into and leverage the knowledge of all experts, not depend on the skill of on-call experts.

One way to make this knowledge available throughout the organization is through runbooks. Runbooks have different maturity stages, as shown in Figure 9-9:

- **Ad-hoc:** The initial state is characterized by individual manual actions with no documentation or consistency.
- **Repeatable:** On the second level, standard activities are documented and consistent across the organization. These activities are still performed manually.
- **Defined:** On the third level, activities are enforced. Actions are made available as scripts and tasks and provided to the operator in context within management tools (in situ execution).
- **Managed:** On this level, the system recommends the right activity for a given event. Using basic if/then functionality, the system executes activities automatically.
- **Optimized:** On the last level, analytics is applied to identify when and what to automate.

When thinking about runbooks, you shouldn't limit your thinking to resolving issues (autocorrecting). Problem determination (autochecking) is also valuable. You might check to verify connectivity to dependent components as part of the automated problem determination process, for example.

Taking a system snapshot is even more laborious. You need to locate the system (hostname, FQDN, IP address); get the credentials for the system; log on to a jump server and then to the server; and perform the necessary commands to obtain the process list, memory and CPU utilization, version information, and so on. These steps can easily take five minutes to perform. If you multiply these five minutes by the number of times these steps are executed each year, you understand the potential of automation. The event management system can perform these tasks immediately upon receipt of an event and send the output of these commands to the first responder. This system has the positive side effect of providing consistent, documented, timely data at the point of incident detection.

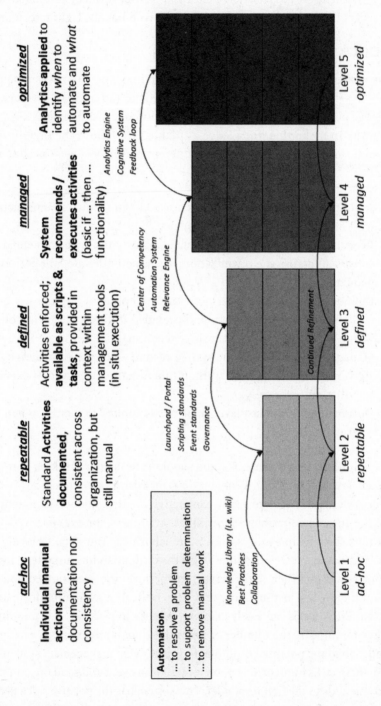

Figure 9-9: Automation maturity.

Over time, these read-only operations give people confidence to proceed toward automation that autocorrects issues.

Although automation is an effective way to reduce mean time to repair (MTTR), it addresses only the symptoms of the incident, not the root cause of the problem. The incident may still happen; it is just addressed more quickly. Following the philosophy of SRE, you want to prevent the incident from happening again. Although the ultimate fix is prioritized and tracked as an entry in the development backlog, it may still be advisable to provide short-term relief by writing a runbook. Also, a balanced action plan provides tactical solutions while ensuring that the technical debt does not grow unimpeded.

Log management

In the previous section on Monitoring, we discussed monitoring of metric data. An additional perspective on monitoring comes from an application-centric view: log monitoring. Developers use logs to record the functional and non-functional behavior of an application by showing individual transactions and exceptions. Transaction identifiers enable developers to stitch together logs from multiple distributed components to get an accurate view of the transaction path through the system.

Therefore, your monitoring solution needs to take application and system logs into account and to consider multiple scenarios, such as:

- Parsing logs for critical entries to generate alerts
- Enabling search in support of incident investigation and RCA
- Aggregating and combing logs from multiple distributed components for auditing and compliance purposes

Dashboards

All the tools we have discussed so far include tailored consoles, or *dashboards*. Systemwide visibility is often needed in addition to specific views. Dashboards combine and link views from multiple components, frequently combining business and technical data to provide additional business context.

Dashboards are always role- or persona-specific. The information needs of a first responder are different from those of an incident commander or an availability manager. A customized dashboard showing relevant data should support each role.

Often, what is missing is not the details, but the context. Dashboards should provide an aggregated view without trying to replace existing product-level user interfaces. When detail is needed, however, the dashboard should zoom in to the details of any tool.

Ticketing

Many enterprise clients require an audit trail of any incident that affects customers. This audit trail should include the times when the incident started and when it was resolved, as well as any major updates related to the incident.

This repository of major incidents enables analysis of trends if the same incident patterns recur across applications.

You can update tickets automatically by linking event management, collaboration, and ticketing, which gives you the best of both worlds: the agility of modern collaborative solutions and the auditing capabilities of traditional ticketing solutions.

By integrating event management, log monitoring, runbooks, dashboards, and ticketing, you have a complete tool chain for incident management, depicted in Figure 9-10.

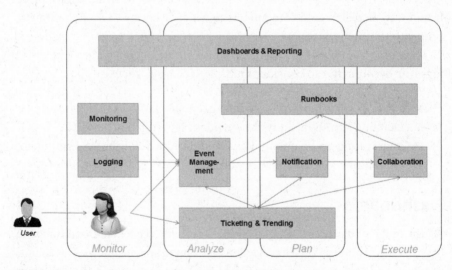

Figure 9-10: Advanced tool chain for incident management.

Chapter 5 introduced the IBM Cloud Architecture Center,[6] which provides practices for building apps on the cloud. The architecture center also contains reference architectures for service management, describing the elements in more detail. Finally, it provides code on GitHub. Figure 9-11 shows the reference architecture for incident management.

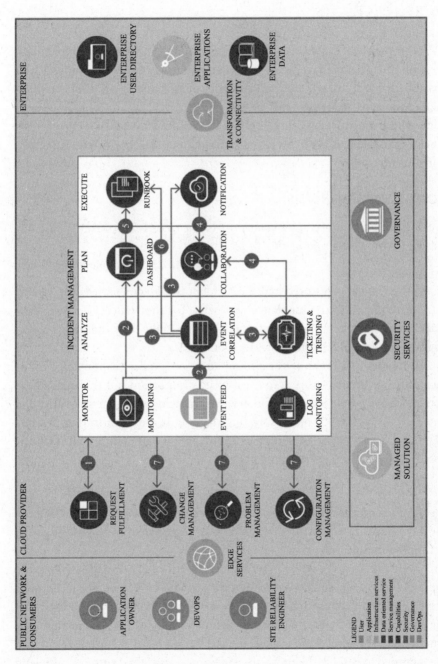

Figure 9-11: Reference architecture for incident management.

Root-Cause Analysis and Postmortems

A clear separation exists between incident management and problem management. Incident management focuses on restoring the service as quickly as possible through restarts, rollbacks, workarounds, and so on. Problem management aims to resolve the root causes of incidents to minimize their adverse effect and prevent recurrence. Both traditional ITSM and cloud-oriented service management agree on this separation, but they approach it in subtly different ways.

Root-cause analysis

Every defect is a treasure, if the company can uncover its cause and work to prevent it across the corporation.

— *Kilchiro Toyoda, founder of Toyota*

When the service is restored and the incident is closed, a series of follow-up activities to identify the incident's root cause (or root causes) needs to take place. You can take proper countermeasures to make sure that the incident doesn't reoccur only if you know the root cause.

The incident commander or site reliability engineer responsible for the incident coordinates these activities, so it is important not to overload the person with multiple incidents; otherwise, problem-management quality and outcome will suffer. To make sure that the details are fresh in that person's mind, the best practice is to remove him from on-call assignment until the post-incident activities are completed.

5 Whys

We recommend a technique called the *5 Whys* to get down to the root cause of the issues and dig below the surface to make sure that you address the cause, not the symptoms.

5 Whys is an iterative, interrogative technique used to explore the cause-and-effect relationships underlying a particular problem. The technique's primary goal is to determine the root cause of a defect or problem by repeating the question "Why?" Each answer forms the basis of the next question. The 5 in the name derives from an anecdotal observation of the number of iterations needed to resolve the problem. Sometimes, four iterations are sufficient; sometimes, you need six or seven.

Following is an example of a 5 Whys example:

1. *Why did the service go down?*
   Because the database became locked
2. *Why did it become locked?*
   Because there were too many database writes
3. *Why were we doing too many database writes?*
   Because this was not foreseen, and it wasn't load tested
4. *Why wasn't that change load tested?*
   Because we don't have a development process set up for when we should load test changes
5. *Why don't we have a development process for when to load test?*
   We've never done too much load testing and are hitting new levels of scale

Not all problems have a single root cause. To uncover multiple root causes, you must repeat the approach, asking a different sequence of questions each time.

Another important topic to consider is that you shouldn't end with human error as a root cause; instead, that's where you should start your investigation. Another technique is to ask "How" instead of "Why."

As we described in the section on cultural changes, a culture of blameless postmortems is critical for revealing all the details of what happened. People will share mistakes to help prevent others from making the same mistakes only if they can do so without fear of punishment and reprimands.

Balanced action plan

When you have identified the root causes, you can identify proper counter-measures to make sure that similar incidents do not reoccur. The goal should be to prevent issues in the first place, but typically, these actions are the most expensive ones in terms of time as well as implementation. Therefore, you should develop near-term fixes in addition to strategic improvements.

Formulate a balanced action plan that consists of actions that fall into any of these categories:

- **Detective:** Improvements are provided to the monitoring and instrumentation components to detect the issue faster. (Example: Add monitors with thresholds that support early detection.)
- **Investigative:** Improvements are provided to perform faster incident isolation and diagnosis. (Example: Improve logging to document input and output of API calls.)

- **Corrective:** Improvements are provided to correct malfunctions faster. (Example: Use runbooks that automatically reroute traffic.)
- **Preventive:** Improvements are provided to the underlying application code and/or architecture. (Example: Perform input validation.)

To make the solution more robust, balance the actions between the provider and consumer of the failing service:

- The service provider should take preventive measures so that the issue doesn't happen again.
- The service consumer should implement additional fault-tolerance measures so that the consuming application is less affected by disruption of the service (by using the Circuit Breaker pattern, for example).

You must add these items to the application backlog and prioritize them accordingly. For high-severity issues, these nonfunctional backlog items should have the highest priority, above any functional feature items. Giving them a lower priority is an implicit acknowledgement that it is okay for the same incidents to reoccur.

Technical debt

There is a risk that some tactical backlog items will be addressed while the more strategic items will be deprioritized time and time again.

Technical debt is a concept that reflects the implied cost of additional rework caused by choosing an easy solution instead of a better approach that would take longer.

We recommend that you measure and review the burn rate of incident-related actions and progress toward reducing the technical debt of those actions.

Executive buy-in and support are required to resolve the conflicting goals of velocity and reliability. As a chief financial officer owns the financial debt of the company, the chief information officer should own the technical debt of the firm.

Postmortem

After you answer the 5 Whys and develop a balanced action plan, thoroughly document the incident, and share it openly.

The documentation typically follows this outline:

- **What happened?** A timeline of events and the effect on the users of the service
- **Why did it happen?** The result of the 5 Whys
- **What was the resolution?** The immediate action taken to restore the service
- **What countermeasures will be taken?** The balanced action plan

Formal postmortem documentation such as the example in Figure 9-12 is usually provided only in a business-to-business context. For end-user services, the information is conveyed more informally, perhaps in an email or blog post. Make sure that you use honest language and admit failure. You must be believed to be heard!

PR2645 - Intermittence on the Order detail screen for Service XXX for REGION

Incident	Severity	Actual Start	Actual Finish	Duration	SLA Impacted	Root Cause Category	Problem Analyst
IN136038	3	02/May/2017 12:00	02/May/2017 13:00	1 Hr 48 Mins	None	Failure in Cloud backend	YYY Application team

Business/Customer Impact

Delay in obtain information, search and modified orders trough mobile devices in REGION

Root Cause

One of the five (source of 20% failure observation) API gateways in the load balancer group did not receive the catalog metadata in a timely manner due to a DB latency situation occurring

Resolution

Adjusting the DB tuning to avoid this latency situation

Monitoring & Alerts

Event detected by APM monitoring console

Major Event Chronology

02/May/2017 (Hrs. CDT)	Event
12:00	Incident management receives the report of the XXX failure and generates Incident IN136038.
12:05	XXX Specialists were engaged in order to troubleshoot.
12:20	Specialists identified that the API connect has an unexpected failure causing the intermittence.
12:40	Specialists identified a particular API Gateway facing issues.
13:00	To restore the service into normal operation, specialists took the affected API Gateway from the Load Balancer group and redeployed the API connect in the production environment.

Figure 9-12: Example of a postmortem summary.

Share the postmortem documentation with affected users after that documentation is developed and reviewed. You may want to share it beyond the affected users. Making the documentation available more widely allows the organization to learn from the experience and prevent similar incidents elsewhere. You can take the culture of transparency one step further by sharing these documents openly on the Internet. Good examples are GitLabs,[7] Cloudflare,[8] and Monzo.[9]

Frequently, SLAs exist on the creation of documentation after a major incident (such as three days for intermediate postmortem documentation and ten days for final documentation). But even without defined SLAs, users expect a timely explanation of what happened and what will be done to prevent it from happening again.

Deployment, Release Management, and Change Management

In a cloud-oriented environment, you frequently deploy new versions of an application into production. Some companies deploy new versions multiple times a week; others deploy multiple times a day. This differs significantly from the traditional waterfall approach to change, deployment, and release management. In the next section, we look at deployment.

Deployment

Continuous delivery (CD) is the practice of building and deploying software so that it can be released into production at any time. A truism of software development is that development and deployment cycle times keep growing shorter. In the early days of computers, when programs were entered in binary fashion with switches and toggles, entering a program was a time-consuming, error-prone process. Later, editing became instantaneous, but compile times measured in hours were common. Later still, modern compilers and languages such as Java and Ruby enabled code to be compiled as quickly as the programmer could save the source file.

Continuous integration to continuous delivery

For many years, it was normal for developers to code their own aspects of the system in isolation while an automated or semiautomated build system ran each night to integrate all that work. Developers lived in fear of being "the one who broke the build", as a build failure couldn't be resolved until the next night. Many teams awarded trophies such as cardboard cutouts of obnoxious movie characters or funny hats to the people who were responsible for build failure.

That approach began to change with the introduction of continuous integration (CI) tools and practices. When code was integrated more frequently, the possibility of a misunderstanding that might lead to a build-breaking problem became less common. In addition, the consequences of breaking a build with a faulty automated test became less severe. Again, the focus shifted. Many teams have implemented CI tools but still do system releases on a quarterly or biyearly basis.

Frequent small releases: Releases become boring

Why do enterprises and commercial software companies put themselves through the pain and anxiety of big-bang releases? Probably the biggest reason is inertia. Operations teams carefully define their operations environments and tweaked them in just the right way to ensure that the environments are secure, perform well, and are reliable. But as a result, operations team members live in fear of change because change might wreck all the work that went into their carefully constructed environments.

In commercial software, sales and marketing teams are used to twice-per-year training seminars, around which they plan their years. In enterprise development shops, the calendar revolves around planned code freezes, planned vacations that respect those code freezes, and various audits and checks that are the usual cause of the freezes. If you turned all that calendar planning on its head, having more frequent, smaller releases instead of multiple large, disruptive releases, you would see several advantages:

- If you change less with each release, the release can break fewer things, which makes the release more predictable and probably easier to roll back.
- If you release more frequently, you vastly reduce the time between concept and rollout. In infrequent releases, the market forces that a feature was designed to address often change by the time the product is released.
- You save time, anxiety, and money by having fewer meetings to plan big-bang releases.
- You have less complexity to manage at the time of releases.
- You spend less time testing and verifying each release.

The benefits are huge. Your team can be more productive, less stressed, and more focused on feature delivery. In fact, when you do releases often enough, they become predictable and even boring. To take advantage of these benefits, however, you have to embrace a few principles of CD.

Principles of continuous delivery

We've shown that continuous delivery is a valuable approach. In order to implement it successfully, you must follow this set of principles:

- **Every change must be releasable.** That principle hides a deep set of practices that influences the way that your development and operations teams interact. If every change is releasable, it has to be self-contained. Change artefacts include things such as user documentation, operations runbooks, and information about what changed and how for audits and traceability. No one gets to procrastinate.

- **Code branches must be short-lived.** A common CI practice is the notion of short-lived code branches. If you branch your code from the main trunk, that branch must live for only a short period before it is merged back into the trunk in preparation for the next release. If your releases occur weekly or daily, the amount of time that a developer or team can spend working in a branch is limited.

- **Deliver through an automated pipeline.** The real trick to achieving CD is using an automated delivery pipeline. A well-constructed delivery pipeline can ensure that all your code releases are moved into your test and production environments in a repeatable, orderly fashion.

- **Automate almost everything.** Just as the secret of CD is assembling a reliable delivery pipeline, the key to building a good delivery pipeline is automating nearly everything in your development process. Automate not only builds and code deployments, but also the processes of constructing new development, test, and production environments. If you get to the point of treating infrastructure as code, you can treat infrastructure changes as code releases making their way through the delivery pipeline.

- **Aim for zero downtime.** To ensure the availability of an application during frequent updates, teams should implement blue-green deployments. In a blue-green deployment, when a new function is pushed to production, it is deployed to an instance that isn't the actual running instance. After you validate the new application instance, you map the public URL to the new instance of the application.

Release management

The concept of CD enables frequent small releases. The architecture of cloud-enabled applications provides further steps that ease and automate the release to production.

Blue-green deployments

As a cloud-enabled application is front-gated by a load-balancer that receives all requests, the load balancer can deploy applications with near-zero downtime. While the current version of the application (the blue version) is being served by the load balancer, the next version of the application (the green version) can be deployed silently into another environment. Final tests can be performed against the deployed green environment without affecting the production environment. When these tests pass, the load balancer is reconfigured to route the traffic to the green environment. New requests will be served by the new environment, and slowly, the old environment can be retired.

This type of deployment, called *blue-green deployment,* also provides an effective way to roll back. Instead of deleting the old environment, you keep that environment dormant. If you detect a problem with the new environment you simply instruct the load balancer to route the traffic to the old, blue environment.

When you change interfaces, you must ensure that they are backward- and forward-compatible to ensure that rolling back is a safe operation. The same is true of schema changes to databases. Our recommended practice is to separate the deployment of schema changes from application upgrades.

Canary testing and feature toggles

You can also use blue-green deployment to switch over gradually instead of all at once. A canary release rolls out a change to only a subset of users. Like a canary in a coal mine, that subset of users serves as a test bed for the new release. This technique reduces the risk of introducing a defect to all users. When you are satisfied with the result, the canary release can scale up and roll out the release to the entire user community.

Feature toggles provide a means to introduce a new feature silently into production. The new feature becomes active only when the toggle is switched on. This strategy contains risk in frequent release rollouts and especially effective if changes are introduced over multiple releases.

Roll forward

Very mature environments sometimes follow an aggressive strategy of rolling forward instead of rolling back. Rather than fixing a problem in the current version, the fix will be applied to the new version and in turn released. Obviously, this strategy can be performed only in mature environments that already perform multiple releases a day. In such environments, the line between incident and problem management starts to blur.

Rolling forward is not always possible, such as for a fix that takes a long time to develop and test. Therefore, rollback always needs to be available. A roll-forward strategy cannot be used in the absence of a rollback strategy.

Change management

Despite all the advancements in automation, deployments and releases still need to be done with care. The IT Process Institute's Visible Ops Handbook[10] reports that 80 percent of unplanned outages occur due to ill-planned changes made by administrators (operations staff) or developers.

Through advancements in continuous integration, testing, and deployment, the focus of a CAB can shift from assessing individual changes to assessing automation policies. As suggested by ITIL, standard changes can be performed without the CAB's being involved. The CAB should establish policies (such as thresholds for code coverage in testing and test results), and based on these policies, the majority of changes can be handled automatically as part of a delivery pipeline. These changes are implemented instantaneously and not slowed artificially by fixed release dates.

More disruptive changes may still require the involvement of the CAB. These changes could occur because the blast radius of a change is large or a disruptive application change is introduced. Those changes should be carefully promoted into production.

Modern DevOps analytics tools can assess the criticality of a change. The wealth of data in code repos, issue-tracking systems, and build systems can be used to deliver apps faster and with greater quality. Examples of such analysis are

- **Developer insights:** Key information on error-prone files, commitments, issues, and lines of code changed.
- **Team dynamics:** The interaction of DevOps teams through the code changes that are being made.

- **Deployment risk:** Information about how code coverage, tests, and security scans are meeting policy and data sent to gates to improve the quality of deployments.
- **Delivery insights:** Deployment data filtered by application, environment, components, and date range that allows teams to view applications and discover areas that need more attention.
- **Availability insights:** Quality metrics (such as service availability and customer impact, RCA action item closure, and effect on MTTR) that enable teams to understand how their applications are performing in production.

Configuration Management

The final section of this chapter looks at configuration management. As you will see, these aspects are still relevant in a cloud-oriented service management solution, especially in regulated industries.

Cloud environments (dynamic, service-aware, increasingly complex, heterogeneous, and hybrid) create the following challenges:

- Refactoring complex, interconnected applications and data
- Maintaining performance and SLA requirements for applications, data, and integrations
- Multiprovider shared-responsibility models for security and compliance
- Integration, data management, service assurance, and governance across multiple cloud providers
- Rapidly evolving technology choices (such as PaaS) and concerns about vendor lock-in
- Organizational and cultural changes to adopt DevOps transformations

Consider microservices as an example. Microservices are loosely coupled and distributed. Applications are made up of many small, independent, yet interdependent pieces. Each component is deployed and managed dynamically. These aspects put a lot of stress on configuration management to maintain an accurate, complete view of the environment.

Configuration management identifies, controls, and maintains all elements in the IT infrastructure (often called configuration items). The purpose of configuration management is to maintain the integrity of the configuration item employed in systems and infrastructure and to provide accurate information about configuration items and their relationships. Many processes (such as incident, change, and capacity management) depend on this information.

CI/CD enables a rapid flow of features into production. At that point, it becomes increasingly important for operation teams to easily and effectively correlate performance and stability issues with application and configuration changes.

The following sections look at some key aspects of configuration management.

Configuration items and relationships

A configuration item in the cloud can't be a physical asset such as a server or router, as these assets are opaque to the user of a cloud service. Instead, the configuration item needs to be more inclusive, containing logical aspects such as a virtual system, container, or microservice, as well as a service.

As applications become increasingly complex, relationships between the logical configuration items are vitally important to provide an understanding of the dependencies, as well as cause-effect-relationships.

CMDB/CMS

Configuration management databases (CMDBs, called configuration management systems [CMS] in the latest version of ITIL) are databases with a well-defined schema to support service management. Given the evolving scope of configuration items, any static data model will have its limits. By now, most CMDBs support virtual systems, and some support containers, but not all support microservices or sidecars and function as service components.

The same is true of relationships between configuration elements. Traditional relationship types (such as runs-on, provides-power-for, and is-child-of) are of limited use in the cloud. New architectures and concepts demand new relationship types.

DevOps tools, for example, can send notification triggers — so-called deployment markers — to management systems, enabling them to track when a change created a problem. These deployment markers could then become configuration items with relationships to other configuration items.

Given the rapid evolution of cloud environments, a dynamic data model is needed that can be extended easily as technology evolves.

For both configuration items and relationships, time is an important attribute. Because constant change, autoscaling, redundancy, and velocity are inherent aspects of the architecture, the system configuration reflected in the CMDB is current for only a short period. It can and will change by the minute.

To provide value in the service management processes, the CMDB needs to look at the configuration at a particular time, such as the configuration of the entire system at the time when the incident was detected. Despite any efforts made to increase speed, the incident investigation and triage will occur minutes after the incident occurs. Time is critical in many other scenarios, such as performance management, capacity management, RCA, and system tuning.

A cloud-enabled CMDB needs to provide a time machine that lets you play back the configuration at any point in time. This playback applies to configuration items as well as relationships.

Increasing configuration item scope, relationship scope, and time as another dimension calls out another need: scalability. Whereas traditional CMDBs can scale to millions of objects, a cloud-enabled CMDB needs to scale to billions of objects. What makes scalability a key concern is not so much the ability to store that many objects, but the ability to efficiently traverse complex relationship trees.

New database technologies such as graph databases provide scalability and rapid model extensions without enforcing a strict schema. Early examples of applying graph technology to CMDB exist, and we expect this trend to become a major one in configuration management going forward.

Discovery

In cloud-oriented environments, the instantiation of applications is dynamic. Autoscaling of applications provisions new instances on demand and decomposes surplus instances when they are no longer needed. Cluster managers such as Kubernetes[11] perform this activity automatically. Traditional approaches of populating a CMDB through discovery and scanning technologies are not viable in an environment that changes frequently. The risk of configuration drift and staleness is too high to effectively support other service management activities.

Luckily, automation provides an alternative solution that can be much more effective. As the provisioning of resources is driven by software (infrastructure as code), the associated deployment scripts can be enhanced to automatically update the CMDB with new information (new instances, additional relationships, attributes, and so on). Decommissioning of a service updates the CMDB accordingly.

Another strategy is to not store stale data in a CMDB, but refer it directly to the element manager (such as the cluster manager) when needed. Although this approach is very effective for current activities, it has some shortcomings. When you need to query the historical configuration or status, for example, this information may not be available from the element manager, which has a view of only the current state. This fact makes incident investigation and capacity management challenging. Also, you frequently need to differentiate between current and future states, and relying on the same source for both views makes differentiation challenging.

Summary

In this chapter, we looked at the transformation of service management toward cloud. This far-reaching transformation affects established roles, processes, technologies, and culture. Based on our experience interacting with clients, we provided examples for each of these aspects.

We described the impact of this transformation to important operational processes such as Incident Management, Root-Cause Analysis, Deployment, and Release Management and discussed the underlying principles and capabilities.

When we discussed future roles, we provided some thoughts on how a future organization may combine and align the two approaches of DevOps and Site Reliability Engineering.

While all these changes may be quite disruptive to the traditional ITIL-oriented operations organization, it is important to remember that both approaches are accomplishing the same goals: Deliver reliable services to the users at justifiable costs.

With this, we now proceed to the last chapter of the book, where we describe the governance aspects necessary to ensure coordination and consistency across the enterprise.

10 Governance

Cloud adoption and digital transformation are the future of IT. As you've seen, however, the reality is that this future is multichannel, multicloud, and multivendor. The complexity of this ecosystem makes the need for governance apparent. An ever-changing regulatory environment further drives the need for effective governance.

As we have discussed, at this time of change in the IT landscape, leaders recognize that they must take a new level of ownership of their IT destiny and reimagine IT's role in the business. To do so, they must clearly define the decision-rights frameworks that must be put in place and exercised. This clarity is imperative not only for short-term success, but also for sustained success.

In Chapter 9, we showed an example of the typical way to articulate a decision-rights framework, known as a RACI matrix, that describes who is *Responsible*, who is *Accountable*, who needs to be *Consulted* and who needs to be *Informed*. Clear allocations of responsibility allow your organization to innovate at speed, yet with enough direction for disciplined decision-making.

Coordination, consistency, and clear lines of sight across the entire enterprise are critically important. In order to address these issues, you must define and implement a well-thought-out cloud adoption and digital transformation governance model.

Cloud Challenges

Moving to the cloud creates many challenges for an organization — including regulatory requirements, sourcing and standardization issues, and threats to security and reputation— that must be addressed through a governance model. We will begin by describing these challenges, and appropriate responses to those challenges, in the following sections.

Regulatory requirements

As we discussed in Chapter 6, businesses and their IT providers are required to meet regulatory requirements, and the regulatory landscape continues to evolve. In addition to responsibility for compliance, you also have responsibility for accelerated business-value delivery in a highly competitive environment.

You need to balance the pressures of safely delivering on your business responsibility by taking advantage of your service providers, the partner ecosystem, and the plethora of services they provide. You need to strike this balance pragmatically while focusing on your core business without being distracted.

For example, you may choose to use services from an external cloud service provider that has significant experience in regulatory compliance to accelerate compliance management for specific workloads. Using a provider of this type would free your IT department to concentrate on a business-liaison function. In this example, however, consistent governance is necessary to ensure that you achieve your desired outcomes. In the end, regulatory compliance is your responsibility and not solely the responsibility of any service provider or vendor. An approach that relies on close partnerships with service providers to deliver basic compliance outcomes while also conducting regular third-party audits for regulatory compliance is an effective way to achieve your desired outcome while not taking on the full burden of compliance implementation.

Sourcing and standardization issues

Properly managed multicloud hybrid environments can provide significant business advantages. Without the right governance and management structures in place, however, you can significantly increase costs, create security and compliance exposures, and misalign with business priorities.

The growing number of vendors and providers in the complex cloud-enabled environment also increases the governance challenge, which can ultimately erode the benefits of business agility and ecosystem connectivity in an under-coordinated environment.

Because of this complexity, standardization is your most effective tool for attaining desired business benefits. Only through standards can you achieve consistency in control, direction, and accountability in the multivendor environment.

We introduced the notion of the industrialized core in Chapter 3. The industrialized core relates to legacy systems and processes that keep the lights on while innovation typically happens outside this core. Systems running on the mainframe, for example, typically are considered part of the core. The industrialized core implies service standardization and integration for effective, efficient service delivery. These are lessons that need to be learned for systems of innovation that run outside of the industrialized core, usually in the cloud.

In our experience, when organizations industrialize all their information systems by delivering services constructed from standardized infrastructure, platforms, management processes, roles, tools, and applications, they find that cloud can deliver on its promises in a cost-effective way.

Threats to security and reputation

As you scale, it is important to continuously evaluate, understand, and mitigate existing risks that may be exacerbated and new risks that emerge. In our work, we have identified the following risks (though this list is by no means exhaustive):

- **Cybersecurity threats:** Online systems are susceptible to being attacked; therefore, security policies must be carefully reviewed, updated, and implemented.
- **Data exposure:** Data in the cloud presents new risks of breach. As well as protecting data, controls must conform to the regulatory environment for data classification, custody, and sovereignty.
- **Noncompliance risk:** In highly regulated industries such as banking, regulatory compliance (as well as a specific organization's guidelines and frameworks) must be a high priority in cloud design and deployment.
- **Vendor lock-in:** The cloud stack is composed of many technologies and tools from different providers. These elements must interact and must be compatible for portability, interoperability, integration, and reversibility.
- **Inconsistency:** Systems, procedures, and policies must be consistent for an organization to attain global synergy.
- **Reputational risks:** Although ecosystem innovation provides several advantages, enterprises need to protect against reputational risks through their own practices and controls.
- **Reversibility risks:** As with vendor lock-in, it is useful to understand reversibility implications regarding workloads and data to maintain portability across deployment environments with no effect on the business.

All these different risks must be addressed through governance. You need to consider these possible risks at all levels of your development and delivery cycle through a robust governance process.

Aspects of a Governance Model

Based on our experience working with clients, we recommend a governance model that does the following:

- Enables you to identify, manage, and mitigate risks.
- Helps you ensure regulatory compliance.
- Helps you drive toward standardized solutions and solution patterns in a concerted way. (*Solution patterns* are generalized solutions developed for one purpose and applied to other scenarios.)
- Promotes consistent cloud adoption throughout your organization.
- Drives synergy through sharing and reusing processes that work, captured as best practices.

For such a governance model to be effective, the following elements must be in place:

- Strong technical leadership to define and implement the right cloud strategy and architecture with a focus on exploiting opportunities and mitigating risk.
- An internal operating model that leverages new consumption and delivery models based on self-service, chargeback, showback, or pay per use. *Showback* is a way of driving awareness of costs (through reporting) without cross-charging those costs and a good transitional approach for getting to pay per use or a chargeback model. The goal of these approaches is to promote transparency in the operational model in the deployment, delivery, and management of services.
- Appropriate talent management and human resources policies to attract, retain, and grow the required expertise and capabilities to accelerate your cloud adoption and digital transformation initiatives.
- If your organization operates multinationally, global partnerships and alliances that create collaborative ecosystems and enable your services to be offered internally and externally, aligned with your overall cloud strategy and the target markets in which you operate.

Defining a Governance Model

Your governance model should clearly establish core principles and standards that enable you to govern cloud-related decisions. Because technology is inextricably tied to business, your cloud decisions must align with your strategic business intent and desired strategic business outcomes. This alignment enables your organization to navigate cloud adoption and appropriately manage risk while maximizing value.

This governance model reduces the risk of overlapping responsibilities and gaps that may occur in the execution of your cloud strategy. Additionally, it establishes a baseline for new policies or refinements that your organization develops in the future.

Because each organization is unique, the governance model needs to be defined to work for your organization. There are some basic aspects that need to be part of any effective governance model, however. These aspects are:

- You need to create the right governance structures in terms of organizational responsibility and process.
- You need to define a set of common governance principles that address the potential risks outlined in the previous section.
- You must establish a responsibility matrix defining how to execute against your governance principles.

In our work with clients, we have found the question in many cases is not whether a client has a governance model, but how effective the client's governance model will be in supporting the strategic intent of the business.

As we discussed in Chapter 1, cloud computing has the potential to disrupt traditional technology controls and policies. Organizations that try to govern cloud use or associated delivery models with existing strategies will not gain the benefits of cloud computing. Worse, they may lose the capacity to attract and retain talent to fuel innovation for business outcomes. In the worst cases, we have seen projects fail due to friction created by a mismatch between strategic intent and governance model. A lack of effective cloud governance can create unchecked, costly system sprawl; shadow IT; and increased security risks.

An existing industrialized core requires predictable uptime and tends to have less-frequent technology updates. Note that over time, projects that begin as part of the more agile cloud environment naturally become part of the industrialized core as they are hardened and woven into the way the business functions. With this promotion to the core, more care and rigor must be taken in updates, as these services become part of keeping the lights on for the business. The failure of an associated service or system in the core has wide-reaching ramifications for the business.

Because of this inevitable crossover, an effective cloud governance model must balance these requirements by addressing the relationships among technology users, administrators, and IT leadership, accounting for both current and future IT goals.

The governance model should cover the services you deliver to your lines of business and your end users. It should cover the regulatory requirements your organization faces regarding these services, sourcing and standardization policies that are part of service procurement, and the method by which the IT portfolio is managed.

Considerations for your governance model

In the preceding section, we outlined three aspects of a governance model; governance structures, governance principles, and a responsibility matrix. These three parts are required to be successful with a cloud governance model. In the following list, we provide some additional considerations for what these aspects should accomplish:

- **Think carefully about what governance means to your specific organization.** Prioritize only those policies and procedures that enable sustained adoption and use of cloud technologies so that you can achieve differentiated business value in your governance model. We further recommend that you focus on how you measure effectiveness, periodically evaluate these measures, and make a concerted effort to improve those measures over time.

- **Adopt a holistic cloud governance approach that balances the need for control to mitigate against risk with the benefits of technology flexibility.** Allow for new cloud-native applications that are integrated with external service provider services, as well as existing industrialized core that keep the lights on for your business. You need to capture this balance in the set of guiding principles for your governance model — this may lead you to adopting "multimodal" IT, at least in the short term, but this should be a waypoint and not a long-term solution.

■ **Your governance model should specifically cover the decision-rights framework for direction, for evaluation and control, and for execution and monitoring for conformance to policy and performance.** This model helps you understand organizational alignment, including roles and responsibilities; team reporting and communication structures; and skills required for successful native-cloud application development, as well as skills required for bridging to your existing industrialized core information technology estates, in a multicloud multivendor environment.

However, even the most well-defined governance model is only a piece of paper unless it is implemented in practice. We have found that the most effective organizational mechanism for ensuring that the governance model is both properly constructed and executed to be a Center of Competence (COC), which we introduced in Chapter 4.

Cloud center of competence

There are as many organizational designs as there are organizations. The intent of the cloud center of competence (COC) approach is to effectively accelerate cloud adoption and digital transformation while aligning with strategic business intent and outcomes. See Figure 10-1 for an example.

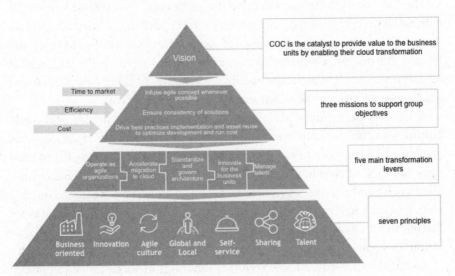

Figure 10-1: Vision for the Cloud COC.

Close organizational coordination ensures clear lines of sight on what is important to a business. In Chapter 4, we introduced the COC, focusing on its role in organizational cultural transformation. In this section, we revisit the COC, this time focusing on governance so that you can see the role it plays as a catalyst for sustained success.

The COC is a centrally funded organization working closely with local design authorities (DAs), which are the organizational entities that direct, implement, and manage design decisions in a global deployment model for the target markets and hubs (delivery centers for these locations) where the enterprise operates. A COC implements three key elements of governance:

- **Direct:** The preparation and implementation of plans and policies to ensure that the use of IT meets business objectives. The COC translates key business objectives into principles and policies, and determines organizational accountabilities.
- **Evaluate and control:** The current and future use of IT, including risk management. The COC evaluates and controls risks, exceptions, and updates to governance components.
- **Execute and monitor:** Monitor conformance to policies and performance against plans. The COC uses metrics to assess governance's effectiveness in meeting business objectives.

The COC enables the units to drive the adoption of cloud by infusing Agile concepts wherever possible. Through its central structure within the organization, the COC can ensure consistency of solutions and identify redundancy and friction that may arise with technology adoption and associated organizational adjustment. The COC identifies and drives best-practices implementation and asset reuse to optimize development and minimize run cost.

A COC is based on a set of mutually agreed-upon principles. Agile culture — a "fail fast and improve" culture — is an example of such a set of principles. To limit the risk of disruption by new entrants into the firm's business, the COC should motivate a culture of continuous change. This culture allows new products and services to be deployed and decommissioned quickly and cheaply. You should treat lessons learned from each failure as assets for further iterations. A COC facilitates and champions the culture of collaboration, customer-centric decision-making, and integration of user feedback.

To fulfill its mission, a COC performs functions in six categories as shown in Figure 10-2:

- **Customer and professional services:** Providing services and expertise to organizational units in the target markets that the organization serves, accelerating cloud adoption, and ensuring consistency in work with the local DA as needed
- **Innovation and partnership:** Sponsoring and fostering innovation throughout the global enterprise, including the partner ecosystem
- **Solution development:** Developing solutions aligned with policy
- **Brokerage:** Identifying, integrating, and agreeing on the terms of use of services in a multicloud, multivendor business and technology environment
- **Marketing and communications:** Selling the vision of the service to business units, key sponsors, and end users; eliciting and incorporating feedback for continuous improvement
- **Platform operations:** Ensuring that the services offered support the needs of the business, with clear metrics for business performance and strategies for continuous improvement

Figure 10-2: Cloud COC general functions.

Chapters and guilds

In Chapter 4, we discussed an engineering organizational structure based on squads and tribes. A key element of this model is the autonomy of the engineering teams. In this section, we discuss how governance can be applied in a structure based on autonomy and independence.

Absolute autonomy never exists. Even with a healthy level of autonomy, decisions must be oriented toward both short-term and long-term goals. Likewise, teams must comply with organizational edicts and regulations. The same is true from an engineering perspective. Optimizing individual autonomous components may affect the soundness of the entire solution or the execution of a long-term strategy. Just imagine what would happen if every squad selected its own cloud platform completely independently of other squads. The result would be increased of operational costs, as the number of operations skills needed would proliferate. This result would also limit the organization's ability to allocate resources optimally across squads and tribes.

Chapters and guilds evolved from the need to ensure coordination and governance across squads and tribes. *Chapters* are groups of people working within a special area, such as front-end developers, site reliability engineers, or database experts. A *guild* is a community of people who have shared interests. The goal of both groups is to share knowledge and best practices. Chapters and guilds have leaders who coordinate these activities.

One of the most important missions of chapters and guilds is to advocate for engineering best practices. Technical guidance and governance should not be applied only through organizational management structures. Instead, chapter and guild leaders provide this guidance through coaching, mentoring, and sharing best practices to build shared knowledge within the autonomy of the squad structure. See Figure 10-3 for a pictorial example of a guild and squad structure.

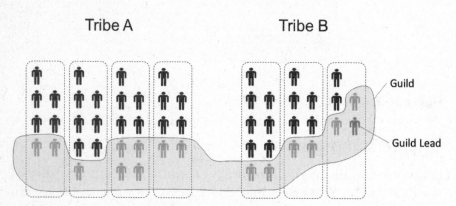

Figure 10-3: Guild cross-cutting tribes and squads.

Still, no absolutes exist; you still have to strike a balance between autonomy and centralized control. As with our recommendation on a COC earlier in this chapter, we recommend that you establish a set of shared principles to guide this balancing act.

A COC and a guild are just two of several models that have worked successfully for our clients. These models aren't mutually exclusive; we have seen cases in which both were applied. Each organization is unique, and we have found that the governance model must reflect unique organizational attributes. When you consider which governance model will be effective for your organization, you must consider your organization's unique context, based on alignment with business strategic intent and similar important factors. However, what we have found is that the most effective leaders learn from the lessons of others and adopt those aspects that have proven to be effective yet align to the cultural restrictions of the organization.

Summary

In this chapter we have shown you what is required to be successful with a governance model for application development and delivery on the cloud. A complete governance model must address elements of risk and must address not only the challenges introduced by the cloud, but also must recognize that the cloud development is fundamentally different from traditional development for the industrial core. A governance model must include a structure of processes and organizational constructs that allow it to execute on a set of governance principles that address the risks we have identified. A decision-rights framework, codified in RACI matrices, is an excellent way to define those responsibilities within an organization and address the risks that lead to the need for a governance model. Finally, we provided two models of organizational constructs that we have seen to be effective in implementing governance in a cloud model.

Conclusion

"Flying by the seat of the pants must have been a great experience for the magnificent men in the flying machines of days gone by, but no one would think of taking that risk with the lives of 500 passengers on a modern aircraft. The business managers of a modern enterprise should not have to take that risk either. We must develop standard cloud metrics and ROI models, so that they can have instruments to measure success."

— Dr. Chris Harding, director for interoperability
and SOA at The Open Group

Keep Calm and Adopt Cloud Successfully

Throughout this book, we have reinforced how cloud is rapidly maturing, how it has become a central part of any organization's transformation journey, and how it underpins enterprise digital strategy. It can no longer be considered an emerging technology or a fad; cloud is now an intrinsic part of the enterprise fabric.

A recent IBM study of more than 800 cloud decision-makers defined organizations that utilize cloud to gain competitive advantage as "Pacesetters." These organizations use cloud to re-imagine business models, make better decisions based on analytic insights, and serve customers in new ways to create winning business outcomes. *Pacesetters experienced almost 2 times the revenue growth and nearly 2.5 times higher gross profit than their peer group.*

Attaining this level of performance means never losing sight of cloud as an enabler for business innovation. Cloud adoption is being driven by business transformation needs and never was about technology-centric decisions. As businesses respond to demands levied by rapidly evolving consumer behaviors, changing business models, and the need to respond to disruption from new market hopefuls and established ones alike, leaders are under pressure to leverage cloud to accelerate a sustained transformation and gain an edge.

Arguably, cloud adoption touches and affects everyone in the enterprise — from the Chief Executive Officer (CEO) down. As such, chief information officers (CIOs) and chief technology officers (CTOs) are adopting cloud computing at an increasing pace to help their organizations face the future with confidence. At the same time, those leaders need to manage such a shift in a seamless manner while operating under increased demands and relentless regulatory pressure and dealing with increased compliance requirements and managing complex Information Technology infrastructure. All in today's "do more with less" and "need it by yesterday" business conditions.

The effect of all that we described above is that there is a sense of urgency, a strong desire to move fast, and in some cases, a rush to capitalize on the promise of cloud and harvesting its potential.

None of us has yet encountered a client that has not made some attempt at cloud adoption. At a minimum, we have observed that many companies have *dabbled* in the cloud. Perhaps they have moved some small applications to an on-demand cloud-based infrastructure service. Their developers may be leveraging cloud infrastructure or platform services to test their new applications before releasing them in production. Likewise, Line of business leaders have likely subscribed to Software as a Service (SaaS) applications, whether IT was involved in the decision or not. Many of the clients we worked with described those early ventures as *cloud version one*.

However, no business ever dabbled its way to success. We have heard our clients talk about the challenges of *cloud version one*. From "Sandbox to Nowhere," to "Runaway Shadow IT," to "Analysis Paralysis," to "Build It and They Will Come," to "Mission In-Complete," to "Go for IT;" all these are common symptoms of rushed approaches.

To maximize its return on investment and the value it gains from cloud, every business, large and small, should *start with an adoption playbook*. The intent of a playbook is not to impose a heavy-handed approach to adoption, nor is it to leverage a "one size fits all" methodology. A playbook ensures that each enterprise can move at its own pace, that each enterprise should make its own decisions on where and how to adopt cloud solutions to meet its needs, and most of all, a playbook ensures a coordinated approach across the organization that will ensure that each cloud decision the company makes to solve today's needs will be sustained and continue to pay off in the future.

The next *version* of cloud adoption is beyond just making different technology choices, altering vendor partnerships, re-thinking operational and management processes, transforming culture, embracing new architectures, laying out a strategy and a detailed roadmap, and establishing a transformation framework. Our takeaway from years of working with clients: *cloud version two* is all about the playbook. A playbook that leverages industry best practices on *how* to adopt so we can *accelerate* the shift from transforming to executing.

An Open Invitation

In this book, we have attempted to share our collective experience, as we have worked to help many clients embark on and succeed with their cloud adoption journeys. But this book is only the starting point of your journey.

We are part of a large community of IBMers, industry colleagues and partners who all have developed specialization in one aspect or many of an adoption playbook. We'd love to see you join our growing community. The members of our team are ready to help share our collective expertise, exchange best practices, and walk alongside you on your journey.

Your first step is to visit our website at `https://www.ibm.com/cloud/garage/adoption`. We have outlined, in much more detail and variety, a number of practices, methods, toolchains, and reference architectures that can be leveraged when forming your own adoption playbook. On our site, thought leaders from IBM and the industry share their latest ideas and practitioners provide their prescriptive guidance.

Last, reach out to any of us. Our community of expert strategists and transformation enablers are ready to help you leverage cloud computing effectively. They have deep technology skills. The team designs, develops, and implements pragmatic, enterprise-class solutions that acknowledge the complexity of traditional and hybrid environments. We can assist companies with all seven *adoptions and transformation framework* dimensions that need to be addressed as part of a comprehensive playbook.

We would also be happy to visit you or host you at one of our IBM Cloud Garage locations. Visit `https://www.ibm.com/cloud/garage/get-started` to find out where we are located and fill out the Contact Us form at the bottom of the page. One of our sales team will contact you and help you arrange a visit to one of the IBM Cloud Garages, or help you engage us in one of our other services.

Notes

Introduction

1. Bohlen, Joe M.; Beal, George M. (May 1957). *"The Diffusion Process"*. Special Report No. 18. Agriculture Extension Service, Iowa State College. 1: 56–77.

2. Image by Craig Chilius, used under Creative Commons 3.0 License.

3. Columbus, Louis. "2017 State Of Cloud Adoption And Security." Forbes. April 23, 2017. Accessed January 31, 2018. https://www.forbes.com/sites/louiscolumbus/2017/04/23/2017-state-of-cloud-adoption-and-security/#310410861848.

Chapter 1

1. Khan, Shahyan, Leadership in the Digital Age — a study on the effects of digitalization on top management leadership (Stockholm Business School, Thesis, 2016), https://su.diva-portal.org/smash/get/diva2:971518/FULLTEXT02.pdf.

2. Steve Zaffron and Dave Logan, The Three Laws of Performance: Rewriting the future of your organization and your life (San Francisco: Jossey-Bass, 2009).

3. Clayton M. Christensen, The Innovator's Dilemma: The Revolutionary Book That Will Change the Way You Do Business (New York: HarperBusiness, 2011).

4. D. Michael Lindsay and M. G. Hager, View From the Top: An Inside Look at How People in Power See and Shape the World (Hoboken: John Wiley & Sons, Inc., 2014).

Chapter 2

1. IBM Design Thinking. https://www.ibm.com/design/thinking.

Chapter 3

1. The Customer-activated Enterprise: Insights from the Global C-Suite Study, page 5. IBM Institute for Business Value. October 2013. http://www-935.ibm.com/services/us/en/c-suite/csuitestudy2013.

2. The Power of Cloud: Driving Business Model Innovation, page 2. IBM Institute for Business Value. February 2012. http://www-935.ibm.com/services/us/gbs/thoughtleadership/ibv-power-of-cloud.html.

3. "TOGAF®, an Open Group standard." The Open Group. Accessed January 31, 2018. http://www.opengroup.org/subjectareas/enterprise/togaf.

4. Scaled Agile Framework. https://www.ibm.com/cloud/garage/content/culture/practice_safe_overview.

Chapter 4

1. "Top HR Concerns." HRO Today. January 29, 2014. Accessed January 31, 2018. http://www.hrotoday.com/news/sourcing/top-hr-concerns.

Chapter 6

1. Regulatory Compliance https://www-01.ibm.com/software/analytics/regulatory-compliance.

Chapter 7

1. Data and Analytics Architecture https://www.ibm.com/cloud/garage/content/architecture/dataAnalyticsArchitecture.

2. Blockchain Architecture https://www.ibm.com/cloud/garage/content/architecture/blockchainArchitecture.

3. Power Blockchain Architecture https://www.ibm.com/blogs/research/2017/05/power-blockchain-watson.

4. "Gartner Says 8.4 Billion Connected." Gartner. Accessed January 31, 2018. https://www.gartner.com/newsroom/id/3598917.

5. IOT Architecture. https://www.ibm.com/cloud/garage/content/architecture/iotArchitecture.

6. Cognitive Conversation Architecture. https://www.ibm.com/cloud/garage/content/architecture/cognitiveConversationDomain.

Chapter 8

1. "Manifesto for Agile Software Development." Manifesto for Agile Software Development. Accessed January 31, 2018. http://agilemanifesto.org.

2. IBM Design. https://www.ibm.com/design.

3. Words and phrases highlighted in bold in this chapter are Practices in the IBM Cloud Garage Method. More information on each of them can be found at: http://www.ibm.com/cloud/method.

Chapter 9

1. "Site Reliability Engineering." Google. Accessed January 31, 2018. https://landing.google.com/sre/interview/ben-treynor.html.

2. "The art of the possible." IBM InnovationJam™. Accessed January 31, 2018. https://www.collaborationjam.com.

3. Weill, Peter, and Jeanne W. Ross. *IT Governance: how top performers manage IT decision rights for superior results.* Boston, MA: Harvard Business Review Press, 2017.

4. Wiggins, Adam. "The Twelve-Factor App." The Twelve-Factor App. Accessed January 31, 2018. https://12factor.net.

5. Fowler, Martin. "Bliki: CircuitBreaker." Martinfowler.com. Accessed January 31, 2018. https://martinfowler.com/bliki/CircuitBreaker.html.

6. IBM Cloud Architecture Center, https://www.ibm.com/cloud/garage/category/architectures.

7. "Postmortem of database outage of January 31." GitLab. Accessed January 31, 2018. https://about.gitlab.com/2017/02/10/postmortem-of-database-outage-of-january-31.

8. Graham-Cumming, John. "Incident report on memory leak caused by Cloudflare parser bug." Cloudflare Blog. December 11, 2017. Accessed January 31, 2018. https://blog.cloudflare.com/incident-report-on-memory-leak-caused-by-cloudflare-parser-bug.

9. Crablab, Chapuys, et. al. "RESOLVED: Current account payments may fail - Major Outage (27/10/2017)." Monzo Community. October 28, 2017. Accessed January 31, 2018. https://community.monzo.com/t/resolved-current-account-payments-may-fail-major-outage-27-10-2017/26296/95.

10. The Visible Ops Handbook by Kevin Behr, Gene Kim and George Spafford, Information Technology Process Institute (2005).

11. "Kubernetes." Kubernetes. Accessed January 31, 2018. https://kubernetes.io.

Index